T0285587

NEHRU
AND THE
SPIRIT OF
INDIA

ADVANCE PRAISE FOR THE BOOK

'This excellent work is a concise, thoughtful account of Nehru's political ideas—particularly on three important themes—politics, culture and history. It skilfully interweaves history of events, careful and subtle text-reading, complex analysis of arguments of political theory and critical explication of moral judgements. It captures the spirit of Nehru's political thought with critical sympathy—both in terms of its politics and its poetics.'

—Sudipta Kaviraj, Professor of Middle Eastern,
South Asian and African Studies, Columbia University

'This remarkable book is for everyone who is interested in India—but also for those who are perplexed by the unhappy course of most post-colonial states. It forces us in the end to ask ourselves whether the tragic missteps in that history are due to colonialism or to the form of the modern state itself. Highly intelligent and generous-spirited, Manash Firaq Bhattacharjee has given us a valuable and thought-provoking echo of Nehru's famous book— his own "Discovery of India"'.

—Talal Asad, Distinguished Professor of
Anthropology, City University of New York

'With remarkable sensitivity, Manash Firaq Bhattacharjee underlines how a truncated modernity causes a rupture in Indian society, which is at once tragic and tantalizing. He upholds Nehru's suggestion that to discover India is to find its plural roots. He argues that the idea of a new India needs to reject historical excess and adopt critical influences from the past, like Buddhism. In this fascinating book, Bhattacharjee shines new light on Nehru's ideas, making a significant contribution to Indian intellectual history.'

—Gopal Guru, Editor, *Economic and Political Weekly* and
Retired Professor of Political Science, Jawaharlal Nehru University

'Manash Firaq Bhattacharjee has drawn a powerful intellectual portrait of Nehru. This is not an "objective" reading but it isn't biased because truth about some matters emerges only when nurtured in a space where two minds meet. Nehru's thought then becomes a vehicle of his own views on some of the most pressing issues of our time such as the politics of identity, majority–minority, democracy, secularism, citizenship and Indian culture. Intensely felt, elegantly written, this rich and compelling book cuts across genres, transgressing boundaries between history of ideas, political philosophy, literature and memoir.'

—Rajeev Bhargava, Honorary Fellow and Director,
Parekh Institute of Indian Thought, CSDS

NEHRU
AND THE
SPIRIT OF
INDIA

Manash Firaq
Bhattacharjee

PENGUIN
VIKING
An imprint of Penguin Random House

VIKING

USA | Canada | UK | Ireland | Australia
New Zealand | India | South Africa | China

Viking is part of the Penguin Random House group of companies
whose addresses can be found at global.penguinrandomhouse.com

Published by Penguin Random House India Pvt. Ltd
4th Floor, Capital Tower 1, MG Road,
Gurugram 122 002, Haryana, India

Penguin
Random House
India

First published in Viking by Penguin Random House India 2022

ISBN 9780670094233

Typeset in Adobe Garamond Pro by Manipal Technologies Limited, Manipal
Printed at Thomson Press India Ltd, New Delhi

www.penguin.co.in

MIX
Paper
FSC FSC® C010615

To my late Baba, Mrityunjoy,
whose partitioned heart was unfair to Nehru

'It was this spirit of India that I was after, not through idle curiosity, though I was curious enough, but because I felt that it might give me some key to the understanding of my country and people, some guidance to thought and action.'

—Jawaharlal Nehru, *The Discovery of India*

Contents

Introduction

The Man Who Discovered India

Two Nehrus

Two Nehrus jostled in my head while growing up: The Nehru in my school textbook taught by my diminutive grey-haired, social science teacher. And the Nehru that Baba spoke ill of at home in his brusque tone, at the slightest opportunity. The social science teacher taught us Indian history in her gentle tone of storytelling. It sounded way more persuasive than when Baba raised his voice to pass off his desperate opinion as the final word. People who suffered Partition had fierce opinions. The ills of history evoke partisan sentiments. It is one thing to lose one's temper with history, it is another to believe in exaggeration as truth.

Nearing the end of his life, Baba revealed that he had once been a part of a Hindu political organization. He left it after he was married so that political activities did not interfere with his conjugal life. An old man belonging to that organization used to visit us over the weekends on his bicycle and hand over printed materials of political propaganda. Blogs with dubious veracity circulate more freely today than pamphlets during Baba's time. The textbook version of Indian history may leave out complicated facts and not offer the whole truth. It is, however, motivated towards an ethic of reconciliation after Independence was scarred by the tragic consequence of political differences. There is a fundamental distinction between society and war. A historical view that professes war has lost the argument. War is not an argument.

Baba was a refugee from Kishoreganj in the Mymensingh district of erstwhile East Pakistan. Neither Nehru nor M.K. Gandhi was an endearing figure for most Bengali-Hindu refugees who suffered Partition. It was easy to corrupt the sentiments of these beleaguered people for political ends. Baba was a good-hearted man, but Partition managed to sever the heart from history.

My elder brother, a student of a Kendriya Vidyalaya (central school) in Guwahati, won a state-level symposium on Nehru in 1979, and represented Assam at the national level in Delhi. The two black and white photographs of my brother receiving the prize from Karan Singh at the Delhi event for winning the top spot at the state level was framed and displayed on the wall of our living room. My father did not miss an opportunity to share his son's achievement with anyone who visited our home.

The Indian middle class can live many lives and have a separate logic for each one of them. Baba was no exception. After my parents retired, the family shifted from our hometown in Assam to the North 24 Parganas, in the outskirts of Kolkata.

The redeeming end to this story is that while writing my MPhil and PhD dissertations in Jawaharlal Nehru University (JNU), I used for research the hardbound copies of *An Autobiography* and *Glimpses of World History* that my brother had won in the symposium. I also used the same copies for reference while writing this book.

Discovering India

In the winter of 1997, I met the political sociologist Sudipta Kaviraj at the international guest house in JNU. I had decided to work on Nehru for my MPhil thesis and wanted suggestions from Kaviraj. Over morning tea and breakfast in the corner of an empty dining hall that overlooked lush trees, Kaviraj asked me how I wished to approach Nehru. I shared my views with him and he seemed agreeable. He told me of an abandoned essay on Nehru he had titled 'The Man Who Discovered India', which, due to some reason, he no longer wanted to publish. He shared some of the ideas from that essay and told me I was free to use them for my dissertation. I was overwhelmed by the gesture. I am using that title for the introduction of this book to mark the memory of that meeting.

Kaviraj shared an interesting idea: Christopher Columbus and Vasco da Gama's claims of 'discovering' India were claims of discovering the other, both in real and representational terms. It was part of the dominant historical mode of Western civilization where discovery meant a natural legitimacy for annexation.[1] In contrast, Nehru's *The Discovery of India* is an inward voyage, an attempt at self-discovery.

The contrast that Kaviraj drew between Nehru's intellectual bid to discover India and the political mode of discovery by Western explorers can be understood this way:

The notion of 'The West', as Stuart Hall writes, is an 'idea, a concept'.[2] The historical project of discovering India is similarly a mode of representation. The idea of the West, in political and cultural terms, is posed in contradistinction to others, the non-West. It is also posed with a sense of antagonism and superiority. In contrast, Nehru's act of discovering the idea of India is a mode of representation that seeks independent classification. It can be read as a marked departure from the borrowed generality of the 'Orient'. The act of cultural self-discovery is self-critical, speculative and evolutionary. It bears the mark of resistance vis-à-vis the colonial encounter.

Despite this distinction, Nehru's mode of discovery is not exempt from the problem that confronts all forms of history writing. It has a political dimension, of mapping Indian history and seeking justifications for imagining (and producing) a nation state. It involves an objectivity where the ethical validity to represent others—within the nation—will always be under question. So how does one overcome this problem?

On that day, sitting in the dining hall, sipping tea as it began to drizzle outside, Kaviraj had an answer: 'We must all make our own discovery of India.'

The Colonial Realism of Perry Anderson

The dubious strength of Perry Anderson's *Indian Ideology* lies in his use of British high-school rhetoric. His half-truths are a desperate conflation of facts. Anderson picks his cherries according to his taste. If you use rhetoric for arguments, you better be giftedly poetic like Nietzsche. Anderson is a realist, who is far from showing any poetic qualities for either language or truth. Here is a sample of Anderson giving us Indian history in a nutshell as a counter to Nehru's *The Discovery of India*:

> Separated by intervals of five hundred and a thousand years, there was no remembered political or cultural connexion

between these orders [Maurya, Gupta, Mughal], or even common religious affiliation: at its height, the first of these Buddhist, the second Hindu, the third Muslim. Beneath a changing mosaic of mostly regional rulers, there was more continuity of social patterns, caste—the best claimant to a cultural demarcation—attested very early, but no uniformity. The 'idea of India' was essentially a European, not a local invention . . . Europeans could define Indians simply as 'all natives of an unknown country'.[3]

The 'cultural connexion' between the Maurya, Gupta and Mughal periods, unlike the 'political', is not to be sought in the official religion or style of their rule. Culture and politics don't follow the same parameters. There is an interesting detail that Romila Thapar has pointed out. One of the seven Ashokan pillars that carry the inscription of the seven 'major edicts of his policy',[4] has an inscription by Samudragupta, the Gupta king, boasting of his military campaigns, and on the same pillar there is an inscription of Jahangir from the third millennium tracing his genealogy: 'three inscriptions in three different languages, over three millenniums'.[5] The pillar echoes a spatio-temporal idea of sovereignty where three distinct elements of India's rich history mark their presence: rupture, continuity-in-rupture and heterogeneity.

Without the necessity to quote historians, there has been the growth of patterns in trade and commerce, oral traditions including epics and their many linguistic versions, philosophical schools of thought, schools of art and architecture with internal and external influences across time, the various Hindu sects, and the tolerance of diverse beliefs. All these facts are *apart* from the codes of law, social obligations and rituals rooted in the caste system. Anderson did not learn that 'religious affiliation' and 'uniformity' are European yardsticks to understand Indian history.

The 'so-called "discovery" of India', Romila Thapar writes—fuelled by the 'fantasy' of orientalist scholars and writers of European Romanticism—'was largely through selected literature in Sanskrit'.[6] The Orientalists invented 'the idea of an unchanging continuity of society and religion over 3,000 years'.[7] The 'material'–'spiritual' divide between the West and India was made by the Orientalists along the lines of Indian life being about 'metaphysics and the subtleties of religious belief'.[8]

This does not make the idea of India 'essentially' European. Europe essentialized India in contrast to its own self-image. Nehru's attempt to discover India is not bereft of modernist, European trappings. It is nevertheless a contestation of Orientalist fantasies about India. The value of Nehru's efforts lies in his attempt to respond to the challenge of imagining the history of a place that was bestowed the status of a nation. India as a nation with a history that precedes it is a modern invention. That is why theories to construct an eternal nation (as distinct from a civilization, or culture) are a fantasy. Nehru does not succumb to Hegelian fabrications by ascribing to India 'a single principle', which is also, for G.W.F. Hegel, a 'natural principle'.[9] The idea of India is not 'natural'. It is derived from cultural history.

Europeans discovering Indians as 'natives of an unknown country' testify to the fact that people did not have a national imagination in the modern, European sense. The phrase 'unknown country' is odd. Does it mean a country unknown to itself? Or does it mean a country not comprehensible to the English? Colonialists confronted people who identified themselves with local kingdoms. The absence of a nation is a political, not a cultural, fact. A *historical* understanding needs to combine the two.

Anderson writes: 'When the British arrived, it was the sprawling heterogeneity of the area that allowed them to gain such relatively swift and easy control of it, using one local power or population against the next, in a series of alliances and annexations.'[10] Heterogeneity is the prime facet of Indian history. The fact that the British exploited a heterogeneous culture by force does not invalidate the value of heterogeneity. It invalidates imperialism. Using the success of an empire as an argument against people lacking unity and force is to furnish a backdoor apologia for empire.

Anderson trains his guns at Nehru's attempt to write India's history: '*The Discovery of India* . . . illustrates not just Nehru's lack of formal scholarship and addiction to romantic myth, but something deeper . . . a capacity for self-deception.'[11] The element of 'romantic myth' in any historical narrative provides a sense of enchantment that positivist historiography lacks. The political psychoanalyst Ashis Nandy offered the insight that 'myths and other forms of shared fantasies' speak of 'experiences' and 'cultural roots' that 'history hides'.[12]

The Discovery is a hybrid text, combining historical account, a social and political ethic, and a narrative of belonging. It exceeds the protocols of 'formal scholarship' to produce a rich and layered work of history as critique and imagination.

Anderson finds a 'Barbara Cartland streak' in Nehru's gendered prose as he quotes from *The Discovery*:

> She is very lovable and none of her children can forget her wherever they go or whatever strange fate befalls them. For she is part of them in her greatness as well as her failings, and they are mirrored in those deep eyes of hers.[13]

The figurative description makes Anderson conclude: 'A mind capable of prose like this was unlikely to show much realism about the difficulties facing the national movement.'[14] Nehru's gendered representation of the nation is sentimental and filial. It, however, has no bearing on Anderson's penchant for realist politics. There is a militarist malaise in the European sort of political realism. Despite the deplorable history of colonialism, racism, two wars, and horrors that European states like Germany and the erstwhile USSR inflicted upon their people, European historians are not cured of this malaise.

Nehru was a realist whenever the question of sovereignty arose in the princely states and frontiers. He wasn't at his best in those instances. At the height of his political battle with the Nagas on the question of sovereignty, Nehru bemoaned his sense of failure in these words: 'About the Nagas I am much worried. This worry is due not so much to the military or other situation but rather to a feeling of psychological defeat. *Why should we not be able to win them over?*'[15] The story behind that admission is complex. It involves realist measures, including the coercive option of using the military. Nehru offered 'a large measure of autonomy'[16] (village panchayats, tribal courts, etc.), but sovereignty was unnegotiable. The political leadership of the Nagas was not impressed by that gesture.

There is no going back in history. If the state is blind and deaf about its unethical use of force, what are our options? It is not a realist, but an ethical question.

Anderson exploited the rivalries between Dr B.R. Ambedkar, Gandhi and Nehru for his bulldozer-critique of Indian nationalism. He reserved praise for Subhash Chandra Bose for 'the dedication and courage of Indian National Army—uniting Hindu, Muslim and Sikh combatants—in battle against the British'.[17] Anderson pushes his case: 'The British knew perfectly well who was more dangerous to them: not Gandhi or Nehru, who were treated comparatively with kid gloves when they were detained by the British, but Bose, deported to far harsher conditions of imprisonment in Burma.'[18]

Anderson's glorification of militarist realism is quite evident. Bose may have been the most 'dangerous' opponent to the British militarily, but the political challenge was shaped by Gandhi and Nehru among others. Even if Bose achieved religious unity in the army, what is more crucial for a democracy is political and social unity. In his defence in court on killing Gandhi, Nathuram Godse blamed Nehru for double standards: preaching secularism for India, but allowing the formation of a theocratic state like Pakistan.[19] On Gandhi, Godse's objection was narrower: 'Gandhi's persistent policy of appeasement towards the Muslims.'[20] Even their political opponents grudgingly admitted that Nehru and Gandhi were nonsectarian. It had a bearing on the secular credentials of the Indian nation state. Their rivalries, often turning bitter, Ambedkar, Gandhi and Nehru were committed to the principle and method of nonviolence.[21] Despite the inconsistencies in Gandhi's non-violence (Anderson calls it 'contingent and ambivalent'[22]), its sincerity and ethical force led Martin Buber and Martin Luther King, men who belonged to communities that bore the brunt of anti-Semitism and racism, to take it seriously. Anderson doesn't belong to that history, and therefore lacks that sensibility.

Politics of Friendship: Nehru and Abdullah

India's democracy faces one of its severest tests in Kashmir. The abrogation of Article 370 on 5 August 2019 by the Indian government took away Kashmir's special status as an administrative and symbolic autonomy that was granted by the Presidential Order of 1954.

Nehru's vacillations on Kashmir were mirrored in his relations with Sheikh Mohammad Abdullah. It had a long-lasting bearing on India's postcolonial relationship with Kashmir.

There are enough historical narratives and political commentaries on the Kashmir dispute assessing Nehru's role in it. I would, however, like to make some brief remarks on the Kashmir question vis-à-vis one specific thing—the politics of friendship between Nehru and Sheikh Abdullah.

What happened to that friendship, in many ways, marked the future of the Kashmir–India relationship. I shall be using Ramachandra Guha's engaging two-part story on Kashmir from his 2017 book, *India after Gandhi*. It is possible to tease out a certain reading of the Nehru–Abdullah friendship from the story told by Guha.

Born in 1905, Abdullah earned a master's degree in science from Aligarh Muslim University but could not find a government job and instead became a schoolteacher. This experience led him to become aware of the influence the Hindus exerted in the state administration.[23] It was around 1932, against the backdrop of growing sentiments against the maharaja of Kashmir, that Abdullah met Nehru. Guha writes that the two men 'hit it off instantly': they were 'impulsive and had strong views, but fortunately . . . a commitment to Hindu–Muslim harmony and to socialism'.[24]

Both had an ethical interest (Hindu–Muslim harmony) and an ideological perspective (socialism) in common. But Kashmir mattered most of all and what brought them close.

Abdullah had been in and out of jail since 1931 due to his confrontation with the Hindu rulers in Kashmir. By the 1940s, his popularity had risen considerably. In 1946, when Maharaja Hari Singh imprisoned Abdullah on charges of sedition, Nehru reached the borders of Kashmir (then a princely state) to defend his friend. The maharaja sent him back to Delhi.[25]

Nehru had, however, managed to register his friendship by that act. The fact that in November 1947, Nehru wrote to the maharaja to hand over the responsibilities to Sheikh Abdullah,[26] is proof that political trust was not based on religious sentiments, but the sentiments of friendship.

What was this trust based on? That is the crucial question. Trust in friendship that involves politics is based on the logic of expectations. Kashmir was the said and unsaid name of that expectation. The demands of a place are not always governed by the wishes of a ruler. The ruler himself is ruled by various considerations. Kashmir was a risky common ground to have as the political basis of a friendship.

In a letter to the maharaja, Nehru expressed his wish that Kashmir be part of the Indian Union but 'through the goodwill of the mass of the population'.[27] In March 1948, Abdullah became the Prime Minister of Jammu and Kashmir. Nehru himself took the Kashmir question to the United Nations in 1948 (a decision he regretted).[28] In May 1948, Abdullah showed clear signs of being with India, holding a week-long celebration in Srinagar, inviting major Indian delegates.[29] In May 1949, Nehru and Abdullah met, with people showering flowers on Nehru in Srinagar.[30]

Guha repeats a point in his narrative that Abdullah showed 'secularist sentiments'[31] in his decision to favour India. I wouldn't see Abdullah's gesture through a secularist lens. His tilt towards India appears partly strategic, with Pakistan looking to annexe Kashmir and India offering it autonomy, besides the possibility of plebiscite. If there was anything else, any sentiment besides that strategic logic behind siding with India, it was Abdullah's friendship with Nehru.

From Nehru's letters in May, July and August to Vijayalakshmi Pandit, one feels that he had a growing restlessness and uncertainty about Abdullah's intentions. Nehru suspects that Abdullah 'has gone to wrong hands . . . and is being misled'.[32] Did Nehru have sufficient grounds to suspect Abdullah? Political friendships are prone to suspicion that stands on the slippery slope of paranoia. Since the nature of modern politics is competition, friendships are anxiously measured against rivals. Nehru was worried about Abdullah giving in to the advice of others. *The rational presumption of the self is such that only others can be misled.* Besides the anxiety of losing Abdullah, Nehru was afraid of losing Kashmir. Behind the friendship lay the place that did not let the friendship be in peace.

In October 1951, Abdullah's National Conference won all the seats in the Constituent Assembly elections. In his victory speech, Abdullah dismissed Pakistan as a 'land-lord ridden', feudal nation.[33] He decided to join India on his terms.[34] All he demanded was a flag and the designation for the head of the state to be addressed as prime minister. Both were symbolic demands.

The Praja Parishad, a Hindu right-wing party from Jammu, opposed it. This led to protests and skirmishes that made Abdullah wonder, in a speech, about what would happen to the fate of Kashmir after Nehru.[35] In July 1952, the Delhi Agreement was signed between the two friends, with Kashmir's special status, which included restrictions for outsiders to buy land and Delhi prohibited from sending its armed forces without Srinagar's consent.[36] Land reforms by the Abdullah government that affected Hindu landowners created cause for fresh unrest. It took the shape of a conflict along religious lines.[37]

This was the moment when Dr Syama Prasad Mookerjee entered the conflict and accused Abdullah's regime of 'divided loyalty'.[38] Nehru thought the Praja Parishad was using 'methods of war', while Abdullah saw its efforts as a determination to communalize the Kashmir issue.[39] The friends were on the same page at this point.

Mookerjee was arrested in Srinagar in May 1953 for flouting prohibitory orders and died in prison on 23 June.[40]

The violence of the protests that followed, including personal threats to his life, made Abdullah believe that 'Nehru could not subdue communal forces in India'.[41] The situation snowballed into a rift between pro-India and pro-independence members within Abdullah's party.[42]

This was a hasty conclusion by Abdullah. If he was committed to Nehru's friendship and trusted him, he should have been on his side against 'communal forces' trying to destabilize the political relationship. Friendship, including the political kind, involves taking risks together. If Abdullah began to have doubts on establishing ties with India (and Nehru), it was the calculative reason of politics taking over the ethical demand of risk-taking.

'It was rumoured', writes Guha, 'that Sheikh Abdullah would declare independence . . . following which he would seek the protection of United Nations against India's "aggression".'[43]

The politics of rumour, the rumour of politics, subverts truth. Truth in politics is circumstantial. A friendship based on political ambitions can succumb to rumour if the terms of friendship are not clear.

Kashmir was the kernel around which the Nehru–Abdullah friendship was woven. It was a place where political fate was open to geopolitical vagaries. Abdullah raised a political doubt regarding the fate of Kashmir *after* Nehru. Nehru, in response, placed his doubts on the friendship. He acted in bad faith. It was a step ahead of doubting Abdullah's intentions; it was a harsh breach of trust. Trust is so prone to the vagaries of politics that even the promise of friendship may fall short.

Abdullah was removed with dubious justification from his post, and put under arrest. 'Why was Abdullah humiliated so?' Guha asks. 'Did he have to be dismissed in the dead of night, and did he have to be placed under detention?'[44]

Abdullah spent eleven years in prison. It couldn't be ascertained if Nehru ordered the arrest. Though it is certain that 'he did nothing to countermand it',[45] Guha concludes from evidences at hand. The friendship that heralded with Nehru reaching the borders to defend his friend, ended with Nehru's silence on the friend's arrest.

Friendship is often a story of shifting borders, more severely in politics.

Abdullah's dismissal under the 'dead of night', and being placed arbitrarily under 'detention', carries the resonance in its language of being a tragic precursor to the fate of many political prisoners in Kashmir till recent times—when the special status granted under Article 370 was revoked in August 2019. The fate of broken friendships in the political history of the world goes a long way.

Two significant details are left. Walter Crocker writes in his book on Nehru:

> It is hardly known, even in India, that though [Nehru's] government kept Sheikh Abdullah in prison, he arranged payment for the Sheikh's son to do his studies for medicine in London and that the young man used to spend part of his vacations in Nehru's house.[46]

'The enemy in the political sense need not be hated personally', quotes the French philosopher Jacques Derrida from the German jurist and thinker, Carl Schmitt in *The Politics of Friendship*, 'and in the private sphere only does it make sense to love one's enemy, or adversary.'[47] A friend's son lies outside the purview of politics, and exists within the sphere of affectivity that Nehru shared with Abdullah. Enmity is sometimes not bereft of affection. Nehru's enmity was political, without being personal. The personal, in this case, wasn't political. Yet it was bound to suffer the inherent contradiction.

Briefly out of jail for the second time (after 1958), Abdullah held long talks with Nehru in Delhi on 23 May 1964. A few days later he attended the funeral of his friend who passed away just four days later on 27 May. Crocker describes the poignant scene: 'Before the fire had died down Sheikh Abdullah leapt on the platform and, weeping unrestrainedly, threw flowers on to the flames.'[48]

The beginning of a friendship that was celebrated with flowers by people on the streets of Srinagar, came to an end with the offering of flowers at a funeral in Delhi. The fire doused their differences.

The Nehru–Abdullah friendship did not quite adhere to Michel de Montaigne's idea of friendship being run by tempered and moderate emotions.[49] Politics doesn't allow such luxury. Kashmir divided the two men, more than it brought them together. Abdullah probably knew this better than Nehru that the fate of Kashmir's relationship with India depended on the fate of their friendship.

Beyond a Singular Idea of History

The photograph of Nehru that I saw in the school textbook, and in magazines and newspapers while growing up, gave the impression of a man who was gentle and stoic. He did not appear to be capable of meanness and aggression. He looked composed and confident. The Mexican poet-critic Octavio Paz describes Nehru with similar consideration in his speech delivered at the International Round Table on Jawaharlal Nehru in 1966. Quoting from *An Autobiography*, Paz says:

> While relating his first experience as an orator and agitator, [Nehru] says: 'I took to the crowd and the crowd took to me,

and yet I never lost myself in it; always I felt apart from it.'
There is neither pride nor humility in this declaration.[50]

There is also an honest admission of detachment. A class
perspective may attribute it to Nehru's elitism. A man claiming to
be different from the crowd is not playing the tricks of a populist
leader. He is not trying to make you believe that he belongs to
the crowd and erase distinctions. Nehru took to the crowd not
to dissolve their respective identities, but to dissolve the distance
between them. For Nehru, class difference did not come in the
way of physical proximity. The writer and French cultural minister
André Malraux corroborates this aspect of Nehru's personality in
his *Anti-Memoirs*:

> I knew that on several occasions Nehru had left an official
> procession and disappeared into the crowd, leaving the
> explanations to the authorities. His tone of voice ruled out
> pretense.[51]

Paz goes on to make an observation in the same speech that I
found worthy of note, when I read it two decades ago. It appears
even more striking today:

> In contrast to the majority of the political leaders of this
> century, Nehru did not believe that he held the keys to history
> in his hands. Because of this, he did not stain his country nor
> the world with blood. For the same reason, he neither offers
> us prefabricated solutions to the conflicts between industry
> and poetry, science and spiritual needs, technology and private
> life. He thought modern society could find an answer to these
> antagonisms by itself. The alternative was spiritual and physical
> death.[52]

The territorial demands of the nation state and modernist political sensibilities led Nehru to use the military in the princely state of Hyderabad, and later, with some justification, to free Goa in 1961 from Portuguese colonial rule. These hard decisions do not weaken Paz's observation when you compare Nehru to the famous dictatorial henchmen of the twentieth century, both on the right and the left.

Nehru was a democrat who thought of issues that were older than democracy. He acquired that depth out of reading Indian history. Nehru, like the rarest of modern western thinkers, had an ambivalent view regarding history. He occasionally felt history moved both ways. The past did not only represent backwardness, and at the same time he could also sense something lacking in the idea of progress. Indian history taught him the value of harmony and synthesis. He felt that there needs to be some humility towards the past. Unlike the West, which wanted to forget its past, Nehru felt one must acknowledge inspiring figures of the past and engage with their profound ideas despite holding anti-traditionalist views. For instance, even though he witnessed the degeneration of Buddhism in the world, Nehru had deep admiration for the Buddha and wrote about him at length in *The Discovery*.

It is perhaps Nehru's deep interest in the past that did not lead him to harbour fanciful ideas about the future, and hold the present hostage in its name. That is why, Paz says, Nehru did not claim to hold the keys of history in his hands. The humility that Nehru felt people should show towards the past, he showed towards the future:

> Whether we were foolish or not, the historians of the future will judge. [At] no time did we forget that our main purpose was to raise the whole level of the Indian people, psychologically and spiritually and also, of course, politically and economically . . . We had to wipe out some generations of shameful subservience and timid submission to an arrogant alien authority.[53]

Nehru may have been an arrogant leader and prime minister, but he doesn't come across as an arrogant political thinker. He was not afraid of being judged.

The most significant *political* defence that Paz made of Nehru in his speech, is deeply philosophical. It opens up scope for reflection:

> It is remarkable that Nehru, in spite of his mainly being a political leader, did not fall into the temptation of suppressing the contradictions of history by brute force or with a verbal *tour de passé* . . . [It] is unique in our world of fanatical Manicheans and hangmen masked as philosophers of history. He did not pretend to embody either the supreme good or the absolute truth but human liberty: man and his contradictions.[54]

This statement underlines a critique of a certain revolutionary philosophy and its reading of history. Paz is referring to how revolutionary politics has furnished us with a total understanding of the world and its problems (bourgeois state, capitalism, class-divided society), and offered us a total solution (communist state, socialism, classless society). This idea, coming from Karl Marx and others inspired by him, has led to regimes claiming to be revolutionary, and indulging in gross State violence in the name of an idea. This has raised grave doubts and ethical questions on revolutionary thinking. It is necessary to briefly explain this idea, as I offer my critique and point of difference.

History, or human reality, produces contradictions. Reason identifies these contradictions. For Immanuel Kant, contradiction is purely in the mind (in the form of antinomies, thesis and antithesis). For Hegel and Marx, contradiction is in the world. Both locate it differently. Hegel finds contradictions in objects as much as in ideas and concepts—in the very nature of reality—hence in (our understanding of) both nature and history. Marx identifies contradiction in social forces. The idea of contradiction in Hegel, despite being located in the world, is held at an abstract level of understanding. For Marx, contradiction defines the forces behind social reality.

For Hegel, the Idealist, contradictions get resolved through mediations within an overall totality of an Idea. A political system—the modern state—is a manifestation of the Idea. For Hegel, concrete social relations are a manifestation of relations between ideas. To treat the Idea and its corresponding political system as a totality where contradictions get resolved is a philosophical assumption to justify the idea of the State. The State itself is always struggling with (irreconcilable) contradictions. For Marx, the Materialist, contradictions in the *real world* (of production) cannot get resolved by abstract mediations (at the level of ideas). The contradiction produced by capitalism (for instance, between labour and value) foster real exploitation. There is a fundamental contradiction in social relations (and forces) of production. Marx identifies the problem in Hegel, but invents his own *real* totality in the name of class. He seeks to reconcile class contradictions by his idea of the communist state.

Marx-inspired revolutionary politics seeks to erase or dismantle 'antagonistic'[55] contradictions by the legitimate use of violence. It ignores the poetic insight that contradiction is 'a law; the very substance of history and man himself'.[56] To reconcile by (class) war what is irreconcilable in history is a disastrous logic of political reason and the crisis of Marxist revolutionary thought. The idea that class alone defines the social meaning of people, that class alone is the engine of social change or transformation, and that class alone determines the fate of history is an oversimplification. Social condition is multiple. Society (and by extension, nation) is not a totality. It is time we pay attention to the more reconcilable aspect in history: *the question of relation.*

Along with the idea of contradiction in class-based society, lies Marx's theory of alienation: The worker is alienated from his labour because he doesn't own or control the means of production. He is forced to sell his labour power cheaply, thus losing the value of his being and his labour for the capitalist's profit. This in turn leads to alienation.

Marx's idea of alienation is real but limited. Capitalism produces alienation related to production, and relations of production. Marx raises the political question of how to erase the contradiction between labour and value. This contradiction is mediated by a power structure based on exploitation that must be dismantled. Marx's theory is totalizing. It offers us a singular idea of history and society that is based on class alone. Social history is more complex and diverse. That is why a single revolutionary idea cannot provide us redemption.

Alienation is not just a problem of labour. Alienation is also a spiritual and cultural condition, not reducible to the problem of production alone. There are also social forms of alienation that are not class-based (like caste, which Ambedkar called 'a fixed notion in the mind . . . a notion that is of a hierarchy based on birth'[57]).

Production alone does not guarantee either the elevation or the fulfilment of our alienated existence. We are alienated from ourselves as sexual beings, from language, from the idea of history that promises us freedom, as much as we are alienated from labour. Our relations in the world are not just limited to class. All relations of exploitation are not economic in nature: those between the citizen and the refugee, between majority and minority, between men and women, between heterosexuals and queer, between people of different ethnicities, cultures, religions.

In other words, *we are alienated in our relation with the other.*

These relations are not reducible to class. The other seeks a relation outside our claims to identity, knowledge, and even reason.

How does one imagine that relationship where contradiction is not to be subsumed but accepted, even *embraced*? How does one live in a world where people by their *very presence*, thought and being, contradict you?

The political project of erasing contradictions by brute force has led to the eruption of equally volatile contradictions. In communist states, it emerged between knowledge and propaganda, Party and working-class interests, theory and freedom.

The idea of liberty needs to be reconciled with the presence of contradictions. No idea or truth-claim can justify the sacrifice of human lives. It would mean the barbarism of truth. Ethics provokes us to think of freedom without violence.

Nehru did not sit on horseback with sword in hand, and rush towards the windmills of history thinking they were giants he had to exterminate. He did not hallucinate from the desire to rid the world of all ills and create a gigantic prison in the name of paradise.

Political Ethics and the Minoritarian Approach

The last section provides a brief background to as well as an introduction of my approach to reading Nehru and the politics of nationalism in general.

Political ethics involves how the relational individual self, the community, the party or any ideologically coherent group, defines or seeks to resolve its relationship with the other—in history, politics and social relations. The demands of political ethics are all-pervading, over social and political life. It involves the question of power, representation, consideration, and negotiation.

Political ethics differs from ideological perspective in the sense that (political) ideology is a lens, or an approach that is limited by a certain theory and agenda. Ideology creates a framework of politics that is suited to its own ends. And that end, apart from everything else, involves power. Ideology derives its legitimacy from its understanding of how society needs to run. That in turn involves an idea of society itself, highlighting what a particular ideology finds fundamental or essential to address. Ideologies imagine and define a world within certain broad frameworks provided by modern political thinkers.

The Marxist and liberal schools of thought have prospered in the last couple of centuries. Marxism offers us three broad perspectives: 1) an understanding of history and the world through hierarchical class structures; 2) a critique of capitalism; and 3) the idea of a revolutionary takeover of power that will erase the exploitative nature of social relations. Liberalism is broadly based on 1) the freedom and rights of the individual, including freedom of speech, 2) formal equality before the law, and 3) a secular State where religion cannot intervene.

Marxism differs on the first two principles. It holds that the individual is primarily a social being and his status is defined by economic and social interests that place him within a class. In other words, an individual must be understood and defined only in relation to his class position. Marxism holds the liberal idea of equality as bourgeois, which does not consider a more historically grounded social equality. Liberalism also does not have any formidable philosophical and political critique of capitalism. At best it provides context-based criticisms on aspects within the capitalist arrangement of social and economic reality. Both Marxism and liberalism do not help us regarding a host of grave historical problems, because these problems lie outside their concerns.

The problem of the other, for instance, which since ancient Greece to the modern West, has been of certain people (slaves, women, Jews, people of the colonies, homosexuals) being excluded from the rights and privileges of the general populace. The idea of a common 'humanity', propagated by Voltaire and the Universal Declaration of Human Rights of 1948, did not address the specificities involved in histories of exclusionary violence. Voltaire's Newtonian ethics, his idea of natural law and natural morality based on rationalist universalism, and his adherence to classical culture did not lead him to be sensitive to cultural particularity. He thought 'Jews have disfigured the truth by absurd fables'[58] and 'Negroes is a species of men different from ours'.[59] Voltaire, like other thinkers in the West who swore by Enlightenment universality and morality, admitted all human beings into the universal fold of humanity without scrutinizing their own prejudices. Any difference (in cultural, religious or even racist terms) that fell short of the secularized, scientific standards of White Christians was regarded unworthy of the new club.

The language of justice in the Universal Declaration was couched in the liberal-rationalist framework (an intellectual legacy of the Enlightenment), where all rights are reserved in the name of the secularized, rational individual.[60] This framework does not address the problem of prejudice and victimization based on racial, ethnic and group identities. What is deemed universal becomes contradictory once heterogeneity (and the real history of difference) is disregarded.

In his book *Orientalism* (published in 1978), Edward Said addressed the problem of the West's Orientalist tendencies among their philosophers and writers, where essentialist notions (or caricatures) of the East as backward, traditional and reactionary were used as modes or tools of representation that served as Western knowledge about people of the Eastern world. This mode of representation has been used to justify colonialism. It is without doubt, an ethically criminal use of knowledge to misrepresent an entire world of people.

The Indian variant of this Western intellectual history of pejorative othering has taken place in the realm of the caste system that includes the outcastes, also called the untouchables. Dr B.R. Ambedkar—the leader of the untouchables, political thinker and activist—addressed this history of caste prejudice in his numerous writings. In the case of castes and outcastes, the problem of knowledge was based on the fixed traditional practices assigned to each caste under the Brahminical system. So, each caste represented a particular practice and would be judged accordingly. This traditional framework of dividing and hierarchizing people based on the value accorded to their mode of labour established a graded system of inequality. Modernity, aided by colonialism, came as a relief and a moment of freedom for people who were unable to break off this oppressive structure. Ambedkar and others belonging to the underprivileged castes and outcastes dealt a blow to this history of othering.

The historical and political other in discourse (Western, Indian or any other) has been a tainted figure, a figure tainted by representation. Because of it the other retains an ethical force as other, as person or people, to counter the history of power, of knowledge and political modes of violence and victimization.

A host of thinkers from the West—Michel Foucault to Emanuel Levinas among others—have made us aware of the inherent problems in the claims of rationalist knowledge, to foster ideas of universality and humanity.

Be it by Hegel, Marx, Descartes or Kant, the idea of human emancipation was placed in reason, without questioning how not just instrumental (or purposive) reason but also disengaged reason as a tool of absolute objectivity was responsible for the dominance and exploitation of the other (who was considered lacking in reason), as well as for the establishment of a 'universal' knowledge of sovereignty that produced hierarchies of mind/body, reason/passion—thus dividing the human self from within.

In the name of dissecting the self, rational knowledge ended up creating the idea of the autonomous, agentic and free self. This had to be forever alert *to* and suspicious *of* human emotions and passions as modes of the supposedly unfree, non-sovereign self. We were left with what can be called the schizophrenic self: always scared of itself, of losing its autonomy, agency and freedom. Imagine the tragic and amusing paradox (and predicament) that rational knowledge granted us: to be a free self that is always scared and wary of being free. We, the 'others' of Western civilization and knowledge, were anyway languishing in the world of the unfree. We were told we were unfree because we lacked reason. We had to choose reason to liberate ourselves.

To Nehru's credit, despite his enthusiasm for the dominant strand of Western thought that championed scientific rationality, he occasionally paused to think over the problem and raised judicious doubts. Almost nearing the end of *The Discovery of India*, Nehru mentions that the 'approach to knowledge in the past was a synthetic one, but limited to India'.[61] He felt the geo-cultural limitation to an otherwise desirable approach that had been taken over by an 'analytical' approach (which is scientific-rationalist) had to now re-emphasize 'the synthetic aspect'.[62] Science made universal knowledge possible, but Nehru felt that the cult of specialization 'has led to a narrowing of individual life' as well as of 'man's labour'.[63] What Nehru suggests for the modern era is that it is able to create 'integrated personalities instead of the lopsided individuals of today'.[64]

Nehru's doubts on the limits of a scientific approach to life have a Nietzschean ring to it. In *The Use and Abuse of History*,

Nietzsche writes that despite the euphoria of the champions of science regarding science ruling over life, he is convinced that it won't lead to '*true life* and promises much less for the future than the life [of] instincts and powerful illusions'.[65] Nietzsche does not think the age of science can produce 'harmonious personalities' in a world where people remain bound to 'the factory of the "common good" [and] "the labour market"'.[66] Nietzsche is circumspect of the systemic aspect of modern life engaged in monotonous productivity. Such a life dulls instinctive capabilities and prevents people from imagining freely and audaciously.

The integrated personality of the modern era is not the man and woman of reason alone, slashing the self in binaries. The individual is also relational, an entity of feeling and belonging. Pure autonomy creates a problem that is peculiar to modernity. The missing ground of individuals vis-à-vis their relationship with culture is based on relationality. The idea of autonomy needs to open itself up to the test of relationality. Reason can't undervalue the test of (critical) belonging. It is not inspiring to define and understand being an individual; as someone who is free only because reason has established its own *and his* superiority over others. An individual is an individual *in relation to something*. It is difficult to imagine the individual in contradistinction to some idea of community.[67]

Nehru's suggestion of the synthetic approach against the cult of specialized knowledge and labour is an invitation to what he discovers as the dominant trend in India's cultural history: an intercultural affirmation of heterogeneity, where knowledge and culture are produced through the historical encounter. The most exciting aspect of this history of synthesis in political terms is that it took place *despite uneven power relations*. It tells us that civilizations of the past, unlike the modern West, did not create an essentialized system of knowledge based on prejudice that made it impossible for cultures to share their ideas on a certain unique and accepted sense of difference. Cultures were open to influence as much as they were happy *to* influence. This porous and open-ended aspect of culture attracted Nehru and he contrasted it with religion.

The approach of political ethics is to accord the other, or the minor, its proper place in history. It is to argue—critically or approvingly—the political and the ethical aspect in discourses, narratives and contexts that are framed from the perspective of how a certain knowledge, or claim, or practice, seeks to establish its relationship with the other.

Since political life is ruled universally by the nation state, the minor figure is almost always the minority: be it linguistic, ethnic, social, sexual, or religious, and also the refugee, the political outcast of all nations that rule in the name of their favoured children, the individual citizen. The minor is most often the group, a collectivity, and not the unencumbered individual. The problem of the minor is, however, often reflected through a relational individual, someone who bears the mark of belonging, of being *someone*. The individual is not disconnected from the community that faces (the dangers of) persecution. The minor is an identity, whether it belongs to a political minority or not, and is always in contradistinction to the discourse of the majority. They comprise people facing violence or opposition 'because of *who* they are', as Ajay Skaria puts it, including 'dissenters'.[68]

The idea of the 'minor' famously emerged from Gilles Deleuze and Félix Guattari's essay on Kafka. It is meant to designate a certain kind of writing that has three characteristics.[69] I am concerned with the first two: 1) it breaks the limits (and logic) of territoriality and 2) it relates the individual to a larger matrix of the political.

Both these meanings concern (and suit) us here: The minor is a sensibility and perspective that is fiercely opposed to the majoritarian logic of identity and territory. It is anti-majoritarian, for by its presence and utterance, it breaks one/ness into two/ness. In relation to the production of minor literature, Deleuze and Guattari mention 'the problem of immigrants, and especially of their children, the problem of minorities'[70]: how to summon the language of experience that creates a new path. The force of minoritarian political thought emerges from such quarters.

The minoritarian approach opens up a new ethical space in the discursive and analytical field of knowledge dominated by liberalism and Marxism. The ethics of the minor is the ethics of difference/otherness and marginality. In a world increasingly relapsing into the dangers and terrors of majoritarianism, the minoritarian approach is a serious and marginal reminder of what is wrong with our political imagination.

1

Colonialism and 'the Garb of Modernity'

On 21 September 1995, a devotee in Delhi declared the 'miracle' that a statue of Ganesha drank the milk that was offered to it. By noon, similar claims were not only heard from temples all over the country but also from temples abroad: in the United Kingdom, Canada, the United Arab Emirates, and Nepal. Debates on television and newspapers[1] erupted between science and belief. The rationalists explained that pious devotees were duped by 'surface tension' and the simple law of 'capillary attraction'.[2]

However, the more intriguing question was regarding what led to the mass suspension of reason. Claims based on religious belief in India are often not without an element of mischief. The mischief is invariably political. In the case of the 'miracle' of Ganesha drinking milk—then Central Minister for Welfare, Sitaram Kesari, accused two Hindu right-wing groups for legitimizing this rumour for electoral gains. In modernity there can be no miracle, real or fake, that is devoid of politics.

The Hindu right-wing interest in the mass consumption of an event like the Ganesha 'miracle' is obvious. This political aspect should, however, be kept distinct from the larger issue of crazy mass-belief. Right-wing politics could exploit the 'miracle' for its own ends because such occurrences gain widespread social legitimacy. It reveals the dormant collective wish of a community to experience something extraordinary outside the rational constraints of modern life. The ennui of our sociological condition can lead people towards such moments of suspended reason.

The Ganesha incident, despite scientific explanations that countered the mass hysteria, marked Hindu society's desperation for divine magic.

Paradoxes of Modernity

Nehru would have abhorred such a scandal. But a scientific viewpoint on the matter is beside the point. Modernity is not an exclusive domain of positivism. Nor is scientific rationality a panacea for the degeneration of the collective unconscious. If modernity signifies the time for scientifically verifiable idea of truth, it does not obliterate the *other* truth that historically precedes the scientific: the miraculous. In the absence of scientific reason, people in earlier times, before the advent of modernity, believed everything that was accidental or unexpected was a miracle. Scientism invalidates the logic of miracles through reasoning. But miracles don't derive their meaning and power from logic.

In a lecture delivered in 1819, the German sociologist Max Weber, spoke about 'de-magification' (German: *Entzauberung der Welt*, a term Weber borrowed from Friedrich Schiller, also translated as 'the disenchantment of the world').[3] The everyday life of the traditional world in Europe 'before the Protestant Reformation . . . [was] punctuated by saints' days, fairs, pilgrimages, festivals, seasons of feasting, atonement and celebration'.[4] Weber writes in *The Protestant Ethic and the Spirit of Capitalism* that

John Calvin and the Reformation, in the middle of the sixteenth century, sought 'to free man from the power of irrational impulses' and subject him 'to the supremacy of a purposeful will'.[5] It led to what Weber calls the 'rationalization of the world, the elimination of magic'.[6]

Daniel Defoe's story on the pandemic, *A Journal of the Plague Year*—published in March 1772, based on the 1665 bubonic plague that hit various parts of the world, including London, also documents the effect of rationalization in the West. Defoe's condemnation of supernatural practices in the novel through the character H.F., a saddler who traded with merchants dealing with the English colonies in America, echoes the effects of Calvinism and the Reformation in late sixteenth century England.[7] The growth of capitalism and the birth of scientism led to demystification. Science sought to drive away every mystery in the world with rational arguments. The overwhelming material concerns of (economic) life led to the rationalization of both life and faith. This process is understood as *'secularization'*.[8]

The coming of capitalism and the Protestant ethic saw the emergence of surrealism[9] in Europe in the early 1920s (among others like Dadaism, Expressionism, Symbolism, etc) as an anti-modernist movement of the disenchanted world. They produced art and literature highlighting our irrational, unconscious impulses and states of being. Sigmund Freud's 1919 lecture, 'The Uncanny'—where he elaborates on E. Jentsch's earlier work on the subject, explains the paradox behind the German word, *unheimlich* or uncanny, which means an unconscious space where something that was once familiar is now unfamiliar, and hence we are 'estranged' from it.[10] The uncanny reveals the source of what is repressed in us. It leads to a host of neurotic excesses, and remains the psychic surplus of modern civilization. Surrealism and its sister movements wanted to address (and affirm) the state of the unconscious that was ignored and misunderstood by the rationalist culture of modernity. These artists and writers tried to recover and produce a 're-enchantment of the world, and reorientation of human history'[11] as a response to the psychological alienation faced by the human mind.[12] These critical events from the modern West are crucial to consider in our understanding (or judgements in rationalist bad faith) of the irrational, the superstitious and the magical.

In the popular sphere of India's cultural imagination, the disenchantment produced a bizarre episode: the miracle of Ganesha. The common sense of modernity had never completely sidelined belief in a deeply religious society. But never before did postcolonial India witness a nationwide 'miracle' that threw all considerations of reason to the winds. It is possible to read the Ganesha incident as a mark of collective return to the time before modernity. What sort of time was it?

It is not the replica of a time as it existed in the past, but a delirious attempt to evoke what is lost forever. The ridiculous is not constrained by rationalism. People are not happy with the death of gods in their daily lives. The daily life of rational choices is oppressive, repetitive and boring. The desire to return to the time of myth, where reason can be temporarily abandoned, is part of the collective unconscious. Something that cannot be explained by reason is what we understand as the miraculous. People are tricked by rationalist politics. The magical world of unreason is just another trick. The social fact is that people believed Ganesha drank the milk.

Nehru, a product of the Enlightenment, grapples with this paradox in *The Discovery of India*. He begins by affirming his modernist mindset: 'My early approach to life's problems had been more or less scientific, with something of the easy optimism of the science of the nineteenth and early twentieth century.'[13]

Science was the sole source of newness, optimism and progress. But the word 'easy' used by Nehru also gives the impression of what is a fact: the optimism for science and the idea of progress was elitist in nature. The idea of the superiority of science was available only to a certain class of people who could afford a certain education.

Nehru carried the optimism for science and rationality so deeply in his intellectual makeup that he could say, 'If the subjective element is unavoidable and inevitable, it should be conditioned as far as possible by the scientific method'.[14]

Nevertheless, Nehru conceded certain limitations to this optimism: in the sphere of understanding the 'purpose of life',[15] and in learning to 'appreciate goodness and beauty'.[16] In other words, he was circumspect about science being able to provide answers to the ethical and aesthetic spheres of life.

More crucially, he pointed out that science despite facilitating the 'control of nature'[17] failed to bring about self-control or 'the power to control himself'.[18]

In a striking passage nearing the end of *The Discovery*, Nehru comes to pause on his firm belief in the idea of progress coming from scientific rationality:

> There is something lacking in all this progress, which can neither produce harmony between nations nor within the spirit of man. Perhaps more synthesis and a little humility towards the wisdom of the past, which, after all, is the accumulated experience of the human race, would help us to gain a new perspective and greater harmony.[19]

The idea of harmony is understood in both political and spiritual terms. Nehru's 'Eastern' sensibility acknowledges the limits of the Enlightenment project. This also appears to be his reflection on the dark political scene in Europe, reeling from war, the fascist uprising in Germany and the harsh communist regime in Russia.

What Europe lacked during the period of 1942–46, when Nehru was writing *The Discovery* in the Ahmednagar Fort prison, was any trace of harmony. What he says immediately after that shows he had a different idea when it came to his own country:

> But for countries like India a different emphasis is necessary, for we have too much of the past about us and have ignored the present. We have to get rid of that narrowing religious outlook, that obsession with the supernatural and metaphysical speculations, that loosening of the mind's discipline in religious ceremonial and mystical emotionalism, which come in the way of our understanding ourselves and the world.[20]

Nehru felt what's sauce for the goose was not meant for the gander. Europe has to be cautious about too much modernity, and India, about too much history. What India lacked was the 'present'. The past was present in excess, in the form of what Nehru calls 'religious outlook'. So, India was ripe for a rationalist revolution of the mind, which was going to be a form of modern Enlightenment in the social sphere. Nehru had a supreme reason for optimism for the possibility of India's change over from religion to rationality:

> In India, because of the recognized freedom of the mind, howsoever limited in practice, new ideas are not shut out . . . The essential ideals of Indian culture are broad-based and can be adapted to almost any environment. The bitter conflict between science and religion which shook up Europe in the nineteenth century would have no reality in India, nor would

change based on the applications of science bring any conflict with those ideals.[21]

Nehru holds that Indian culture encourages an adaptive and open mind. It will prevent, he feels, the 'bitter conflict' between faith and reason that rocked Europe's nineteenth century.

Let us take a recent example to evaluate Nehru's optimism. Just before the launch of Chandrayaan-2, India's moon mission, scientists at the Indian Space and Research Organization (ISRO), prayed at the Lord Venkateshwara temple in Tirumala, Andhra Pradesh.[22] They placed a replica of the rocket before the idol for blessings. According to a retired official of ISRO, the scientists avoided the launch during what is called the 'Rahu Kaalam' or one-and-half hours of (the influence of) Rahu (the ascendant moon) according to Vedic astrology. The phenomenon occurs during early morning and is considered inauspicious for the undertaking of new projects.

The ISRO scientists know better than anyone else the difference between science and Vedic astrology. Then why did they indulge in both? Isn't this a gross contradiction of one's scientific world view? On closer scrutiny, the matter may be a more complex matter of faith. The scientists won't—can't—bring Vedic astrology into the scientific mission. But *outside* the sphere of the mission, there can be space for other beliefs. In this case, the other belief involves religion and it has a connection with the scientific project. And the interesting dimension of the issue can be located here.

A scientific project like Chandrayaan-2, as described by the ISRO chairperson, Mr K. Sivan, had to pass through 'fifteen minutes of terror'.[23] This is the grey zone during the terminal phase of the Vikram Lander, before it touches the surface of the moon. Despite the perfect calculations that set a machine up for a perfect landing, there is a time of uncertainty which scientists on earth cannot control. In the speculative language of poetry, T.S. Eliot offers us a metaphor for the grey zone in the poem, 'The Hollow Men' (1925):

Between the idea
And the reality
Between the motion
And the act
Falls the Shadow

Between mathematical precision and the moment of eureka, there lurks a shadow of uncertainty. This shadow exists despite the calculable certainties of science. Those fifteen minutes of terror are a terror for everyone: the scientist and the layman alike. The shadow of doubt and fear of the outcome is not easy to overcome with reason. Reason doesn't work when there is fundamental uncertainty. That is where the language of faith sneaks in. The spirit of hope is not a scientific one, even if it concerns science. The ISRO scientists made use of the available cultural resources to draw their hope. That resource involved a temple and Vedic astrology.

It is true that the parallel belief system in god and astrology need not be so neatly divided. Any active interest in religion has wider repercussions that include the social life of people in the scientific world. Scientists don't live in a social vacuum.

In India, such repercussions can be disturbing when they occur in the sphere of caste.

The suicide of Dr Payal Tadvi,[24] who worked in a government hospital in Mumbai, is a recent example of how caste is integral to the idea of modern professions in India. Since Tadvi came from a Muslim Bhil community, three of her colleagues, who allegedly drove her to commit suicide, did not think she was worth the medical profession. According to reports,[25] they humiliated her in the name of her caste identity. The law of positive discrimination allowed Tadvi to overcome her social disadvantage and find the profession of her choice. But no law can be a dependable safeguard against social prejudice.

The doctors who tormented Tadvi did not treat the medical profession in terms of universal aptitude. They understood it within the strict limits of social privilege. Caste makes people belonging to the privileged castes, view modern professions through the lens of traditional hierarchies This sentiment lacks any sensitivity for the dignity of labour, and divides labour into 'mental' and 'menial' spheres.

No wonder we had doctors from All India Institute of Medical Sciences (AIIMS), protesting against reservations for Other Backward Class (OBC) in 2006 with brooms in hand. According to the idea of modernity, the expectations that flow from being part of a scientific profession like medical science include a sensibility towards human equality and the universal idea of being human. It is not expected within this world view, for someone to retain sentiments of caste hierarchy. A scientific occupation is supposed to rid people of traditional notions of hierarchy.

In India, the occupational does not translate into a new idea of the social. Sharing a common space with others intensifies caste distinctions rather than erase them. Caste runs parallel to occupational relation. Modern occupations did not create a social ethic for Hindus that is independent of caste.

Modernity brought a set of new values that challenged the world to think afresh. The Enlightenment gave the idea of the unencumbered human being who is free, and who is dictated by reason. Reason seeks to establish a critical relationship with all forms of traditional beliefs that were once held by religion. The idea of philosophical (and political) authority shifted from religion to reason. Democracy gave birth to the idea of a people, which is an idea of constitutional equality. Yet, the West did not give up on racism, and its discriminatory mindset against the colonies, Jews and others. India, inheriting a colonial modernity, did not give up on caste among other prejudices.

Nehru thought that the 'tyranny of caste' will succumb to the onslaught of 'the conditions of modern life'.[26] Nehru's modernist optimism, shared by many Marxist and liberal thinkers in India, did not come to be. They thought the progressive culture of modernity would overwhelm old notions and structures of exploitation and belief. Caste proved to be a stubborn institution, way more resistant to change than was envisaged by Nehru and others who shared the optimism of social progress. They had failed to understand the historical nature of caste and the new shape it may take under modern conditions.

Not just that: Nehru was ambivalent about the origins of the caste system. He saw the earlier form of caste as 'an attempt at the social organization of different races, a rationalization of the facts as they existed at the time'.[27] It is rationalist prejudice to think (in retrospect) that a hierarchical system used to sort out the problem of racial difference may have an acceptable argument in its favour. 'For all its virtues and the stability', Nehru wrote on the caste system, 'it had given to Indian society, it carried within it the seeds of destruction.'[28] Nehru's sociology of caste did acknowledge the social fact that 'the ultimate weakness and failing of the caste system and the Indian social structure were that they degraded a mass of human beings and gave them no opportunities to get out of that condition educationally, culturally, or economically'.[29] This was not just a weakness but the essential nature, pleasure and motive of the caste system from its inception.

Nehru makes an interesting remark that the formation of 'caste divisions, originally intended to separate the Aryans from the non-Aryans, reacted on the Aryans themselves, and as division of functions and specialization increased, the new classes took the form of castes'.[30] This is an interesting claim, which, if historically traced, could help scholars challenge the old understanding by Indian Marxists who argue that class is more fundamental than caste. D.D. Kosambi maintained that '[caste] is class at a primitive level of production'.[31] Liberal and Marxist scholars prefer to hold on to the framework of universal history rather than pay more attention to India's historical specificity, because their value system and political imagination are fed by the ideas of progress in the West. Caste is too backward and feudal to acknowledge as a respectable means to analyse Indian society. They expected a progressive transformation of social relations, based on a scientific vision of history. Hindu society was however, in no mood for such a transformation. So, the groundless expectations of progressive scholars ended in despair.

Dipesh Chakrabarty mentions how the Marxist historian Sumit Sarkar rues that modernity in India turned out to be 'grievously incomplete'.[32] Chakrabarty finds this wishful thinking about a more perfect modernity still to come, as a problem on two levels: a) to see religion and science as 'ultimately, and irrevocably, opposed to each other', and b) to read the modernizing process facilitated by colonialism as 'a bad version of something that, in itself, was an unmixed good'.[33]

Modernity offers both easy and difficult choices, and people have the freedom to choose on utilitarian grounds. In India, religion and science found a strange and discomforting harmony. Modernity opens up possibilities for people to compartmentalize their world views (and their lives). For instance, you can be scientific and traditionalist at the same time. This is due to India's colonial encounter with Western modernity.

In the examples taken here, we have seen how religion and science exist side by side in people's belief systems.

Of Colonial Modernity

The uncritical enthusiasm for modernity by Indian thinkers, as a liberating idea in human history, resulted in at least two unsubstantiated speculations. Firstly, on what grounds can one predict that the historical stains of colonial modernity are likely to disappear in the future? Secondly, has the politics of modernity worldwide always been liberating? The linear idea of historical time and progress has always been only an idea. Alongside this idea, the real world has been living the paradox of progress in heterogeneous time: colonialism, anti-colonialism, revolution, war, industrialism, gulags, sexual revolution and racism.

In *The Discovery*, Nehru makes a slightly different point on India's historical encounter with modernity. He begins conventionally, by contrasting India as a 'static society wedded to medieval habits of thought' with the West that represented a 'dynamic society' carrying 'a modern' consciousness'.[34] And then, Nehru makes a more specific point about the nature of colonial modernity:

> The impact of western culture on India was the impact of a dynamic society, a 'modern' consciousness, on a static society wedded to medieval habits of thought which, however sophisticated and advanced in its own way, could not progress because of its inherent limitations. And, yet, curiously enough the agents of this historic process, were not only wholly unconscious of their mission in India, but, as a class, actually

represented no such process. In England their class fought this historic process but the forces opposed to them were too strong and could not be held back. In India they had a free field and were successful in applying the brakes to that very change and progress which, in the larger context, they represented. They encouraged and consolidated the position of the socially reactionary groups in India, and opposed all those who worked for political and social change. *If change came it was in spite of them or as an incidental and unexpected consequence of their activities.*[35]

Nehru makes a distinction between the colonizers and Western knowledge, but not without accepting the West as the legitimate agent of modernity.

By Nehru's account, the benefits of cultural modernity and social change or progress came in India by accident. It was a definitive historical accident—one designed by the logic of history. The colonizer did not encourage change or progress except to the extent necessary to ease the political economy of exchange (and exploitation) and keep the system of colonial hegemony alive. It involved, as Nehru could see, encouraging those who were collaborators of the Empire and discouraging those who challenged its rule.

It is baffling nevertheless as to why Nehru expected his colonial masters to have allowed the social forces of change that would challenge their own rule. Did he think the British colonialists had a moral (or political) commitment towards encouraging modernity in other cultures—even to the extent of destabilizing their colonial project? By what historical or political logic were the British expected to facilitate social progress in the colonies—that too at the cost of guarding their interests?

Colonial historians from Christopher Bayly to David Gilmour take pride in pointing out how the British institutionalized liberal democracy in India through the education system and the law. Gilmour thinks with benign objectivity that 'British imperialism in India was not always quite so bad as its detractors . . . have claimed.'[36] Detractors are being asked to accept a more balanced picture of imperialist exploitation. Gilmour welcomes former prime minister Dr Manmohan Singh's speech at the University of Oxford in 2005. Without a hint of irony, Singh had praised his masters for the 'beneficial consequences' of the Empire: naming among others, the rule of law, constitutional government, the free press and bureaucracy.[37] Singh did not even care to affirm Nehru's emphasis on Indians having to fight at every step for gaining the fruits of modernity.

This is the perfect moment to remember that notorious statement by Thomas Macaulay in his 'Minute on Indian Education' in 1835, where he laid out the mimetic designs of the empire:

> We must at present do our best to form a class who may be interpreters between us and the millions whom we govern; a class of persons, Indian in blood and colour, but English in taste, in opinions, in morals, and in intellect.[38]

Macaulay wanted to create an army of colonized clones who would help in ensuring smooth administrative and other transactions between Indians and their English masters. Keeping the racial core ('blood and colour') intact, Macaulay was eager to transform the aesthetic, moral and cognitive world of Indians to fit into the political, cultural and economic structures (and demands) of colonialism. The Indian was imagined as a colonially programmed mimetic being. It involves a gradual forgetting of the past. The

Indian who would be transposed[39] into an Englishman in taste, opinion, morals and intellect, was not supposed to serve a deep history of culture. Colonialism uproots people's ties with their culture, and divides it vis-à-vis the colonizer's own. Macaulay's Indian was bound to lack depth, for imitation fails to acquire depth. The Macaulay syndrome is a racially imagined caricature who finds it impossible to be English, or remain Indian.

It is not Macaulay's racist criteria for being English and Indian that prevents the Indian from being English. Rather, it is that imitative gesture written into the script of this transposition that makes an Indian a shallow figure of postcolonial modernity. Nehru has paid attention to this problem. Here he says:

> India will find herself again when freedom opens out new horizons . . . To-day she swings between a blind adherence to her old customs and a slavish imitation of foreign ways. In neither of these can she find relief or life or growth . . . It should be equally obvious that there can be no cultural or spiritual growth based on imitation. Such imitation can only be confined to a small number which cuts itself off from the masses and the springs of national life. True culture derives its inspiration from every corner of the world but is home-grown and has to be based on the wide mass of people . . . The day of a narrow culture confined to a small fastidious group is past.[40]

This is a thoughtful perspective. Nehru feels it is time to welcome the winds of change and embrace the new. The 'new horizon' is undoubtedly modernity. For anti-colonial cultures, modernity comes with the obvious problem that Macaulay sought to exploit to the colonialists' advantage. The idea of a non-colonial modernity may sound attractive as a possibility. The language and principle of administrative, legal and educational institutions in

India will remain colonial in varying degrees till modernity lasts. The tragic irony behind Macaulay's statement is that his intention of producing a new breed of colonized people was bound to be successful, even without any conscious effort by the British. Colonialism is a machine that automatically produces a mass of people who are trapped into imitating the ways of their rulers.

It is important to note that Nehru suggests it is the elite minority that falls prey to the culture of imitation. The reason is its proximity to power as well as the desire to mimic that power. The elite wilfully represented Macaulay's dream. For the Indian elite, power meant serving the people of their class (and caste). In this, the unprivileged castes are right in complaining today that they are worse off under elite Indians belonging to privileged castes who eye them with a prejudice that was absent in the British. The colonial gaze did not reflect the internal differentiation of Indian society. It was, however, not just prejudice but also modes of discrimination that prevailed in the power relations between the Indian caste elite and others.

Nehru at this point offers two distinctions on the authenticity of culture: something that is open to influence and yet rooted to the soil, and something that is beyond the privileged class. It resembles an idea of democracy, or democratic culture. Democracy is a modern system of governance and civic life, while culture is a term that refers to a paradox: it consists of both historical evolution and particularity. Democracy inherits that paradox of culture. The imitation of the master, born of colonialism, adds a unique problem to this paradox. Sudipta Kaviraj calls democracy a 'part of the political enchantment of modernity'.[41] In a postcolonial country, the enchantment includes the irrational surplus of all that modernity fails to structure, or put in order.

Homi K. Bhabha calls mimicry 'the most elusive and effective strategies of colonial power and knowledge'.[42] If we keep Macaulay's intentions in mind, Bhabha hits the nail on the head when he writes, 'colonial mimicry is the desire for a reformed, recognizable Other, as a subject of a difference that is almost the same, but not quite'.[43] Bhabha goes on to lay bare the complex phenomenology of this mode of mimicry where essence is replaced by invention. The ambivalent figure of the colonized (or postcolonized) appears on the stage of modern history as neither this nor that—a doubly inauthentic person.

This is colonialism's most treacherous 'gift' to its colonies. Macaulay's figure of postcolonial mimicry cannot be trusted either morally or politically. The choices, promises and beliefs of such characters are born out of constant ambivalence. They are split between serving (and extending) the nature of colonialism, even as they bring their own cultural and social individuality. It is not so much the nature of the difference that matters here but the nature (and extent) of mimicry. The figure of the Indian oscillates within a spectrum of influence that lies between the received knowledge of colonialism and India's cultural self.

No wonder then that the man of science is not quite the man of science. The doctors are not only doctors: they are *also* believers and casteists. By being both, they affirm and refute their existence as Macaulay's people.

The Ambivalent Subject

The ambivalent figure of postcolonial modernity that emerges from this analysis so far, challenges the so-called 'domain of sovereignty'[44] that political theorist, Partha Chatterjee tries to secure for anti-colonial nationalism. Chatterjee argues anti-colonial Indians manage to separate their outer and inner or material and spiritual domains in the world of social institutions in their everyday form of resistance to colonialism. The outer—

what Chatterjee calls 'outside' or 'material'[45]—domain belongs to statecraft, economy, science and technology, where the West is granted superiority. The 'inner' or 'spiritual' domain bears the 'marks of cultural identity',[46] where the Indian self asserts its sovereignty. According to Chatterjee, the cultural sphere of the inner or spiritual domain, fashions a non-Western modernity. There is an objectivist assumption that modernity allows clearly demarcated spheres of inner and outer within the colonized self. The distinction of inner and outer, material and spiritual is also too neat, or neatly drawn. Be it a personal experience or a conceptual understanding, what is understood by inner and outer, spiritual and material, cannot be rationally demarcated or determined. The separate domains of inner and outer remain porous and in excess of what we objectively try and establish as their limits.

It is quite absurd for people to divide themselves up from within into material and spiritual zones, based on two irreconcilable world views and value systems. The condition looks ripe for a split personality that suffers, in psychotherapeutic terms, from a dissociative identity disorder. One wonders whether Chatterjee took this psychopathological aspect and its consequences into consideration.

If Nietzsche is to be believed, it is in times of an 'excess of history' when 'the contrast of inner and outer is emphasized and personality weakened'.[47] Nietzsche hints at a repressed personality. The inner and outer gets mechanically divided, and the 'cleft between substance and form is widened'.[48] Anticolonial modernity pushed people in the colonies towards an excess of history, and put them at the mercy of the political. India's forced entry into the modern political history was creative and tragic. It was deemed necessary from the point of view of progress. There was, however, no way the complications of modernity that produced a repressed self-identity could be averted.

The colonized do not have the luxury to decisively think and act according to the protocols of authenticity. Colonialism intervenes and corrupts our relation with the spiritual and the material. Instead of being sovereign, the material and spiritual domains are prone to being messy and mixed up. It suggests a case of double inauthenticity.

This is best explained in relation to the history of India's public culture.

Shabnum Tejani has drawn our attention to how Hindu beliefs, festivals and reform movements from the late nineteenth century, in the context of Maharashtra (one of India's biggest regions that have seen all forms of political movements), were organized around a strict sense of competition with the Muslim community.[49]

Cow protection, for instance, was spearheaded by the Arya Samaj in 1882 as part of the 'Shuddhi' (purification) movement, where converts to Christianity and Islam were brought back into the Hindu fold. It included cow-worship, and the prime motive of the movement, Tejani discovers, stems from 'an anti-Muslim sentiment'.[50] The refashioning of the Ganapati festival in Maharashtra in 1893 began as a ten-day festival, 'consciously modelled as a mirror image of the Shia festival of Muharram, in which Hindus had customarily participated'.[51]

Tejani shows how reformers from privileged castes in the late 1880s critiqued religious and social practices among Hindus, like idol worship, sati and prevention of widow remarriage. They also critiqued caste for stifling individuality, and for being a barrier to national unity. The reformers challenged Westernization, even though they sought to bridge the gap between traditional and Western knowledge and ideas of freedom. Secular education was preferred in many circles over traditional religious teaching. Brahmin supremacy, however, was never in question. The reformers responded to the missionary challenge by updating Hindu society and accommodated modern values. That did not lead them to question the caste hierarchy. The reformers spoke against those practices which were either discriminatory (and caught the eye of the Christian West), or those which lacked rationality. They allowed others to quietly remain.

It was a bold move during that time, to argue reforms in social practices in the face of the challenge from modern or Western ideas, while at the same time being alert to the effects of colonialism. The ambivalences are visible. There is a significant transformation in the idea of Hindu cultural pride, where change becomes a norm. And yet, these changes are measured against others (Muslims, Christians). The refashioning of the collective Hindu self occurs in a bid to establish political and cultural hegemony. The politics of culture revolves around the competition for power.

There is a unique utilitarian streak in the story of cultural regeneration concerning the Hindus during colonial times. They did not simply desire to promote social good through mass reform, but also do it with an ulterior purpose: to help themselves be in a politically advantageous position vis-à-vis other communities. Cultural change was promoted with a rational motive of securing benefits in the social and political sphere.

Social change was not just a means to reconcile with the values of modernity, but also secure one's cultural identity and make it formidable in relation to others. The presence of other religious communities forced Hindu society to mark their cultural and political territory. It became necessary to mark one's difference for a double motive: one, to assert cultural hegemony against other communities by proclaiming what practices are allowed and not allowed within the national territory; and two, to compete for colonial recognition. Such are the political motivations of modernity.

There were social and cultural transformations from within. To claim cultural sovereignty for Hindu society in its inner or spiritual domain is to stretch the point.

For instance, Tejani has pointed out, citing Rosalind O' Harlon, that the non-Brahmin reform movement in Maharashtra was aided by 'missionary critiques in combination with radical ideas taken from the European Enlightenment'.[52] It included the 'natural rights of the individual'.[53] Whether it was the non-Brahmin critique of Hindu society or that of the Brahmin elites like Ram Mohan Roy and Bal Gangadhar Tilak, no idea of change occurred in the cultural and spiritual sphere without the influence of Western or Christian ideas. Most changes were propelled by the idea of individual rights and human freedom, where rationality did not necessarily play a significant part. Freedom as a political argument is a matter of the human spirit, which is bound to strike against any idea of tradition that hierarchizes human beings and limits their possibilities. There is nothing rational about it. So, the influence of Western or Christian ideas need not be equated with the dominance of rational thought.

Indians realized they were facing a new time in history. Colonial rule created new structures where religion came into conflict with new modes of life. People adapted to changing values without abandoning older ones. In other words, Indians imbibed the deception of modernity. All social and cultural values were split into not just belief and unbelief, but also half-beliefs. Unlike Chatterjee's neat binaries, the cultural and spiritual spheres of the Indians were themselves split into public and private, outer and inner, where you could never predict or tell between reality and artifice. Modern Indians are an enigma because colonial modernity has split them within themselves.

What the contemporary social and cultural situations discussed above have shown, the modern Indian self does not seem to face any serious crisis in holding views that are incompatible with each other. This is what modernists like Nehru, in their enthusiasm for a new universal culture in human history, did not anticipate. The magic wand of reason that was supposed to rid people of all traditional beliefs and historical prejudice did not work. Reason is anyway not supposed to produce miracles. Reason dictates a form of thinking that weighs beliefs and arguments from a perspective grounded in the values of modernity: universality, progress, liberty, equality and fraternity. The recognition of difference poses limits to universality. Progress can't be understood as either mastery (of nature) or accumulation (of capital).

The French poet, Arthur Rimbaud, declared in *A Season in Hell*, 'It is necessary to be absolutely modern'.[54] He hinted with playful sarcasm at the demands that modernity makes on the self (maturity, objectivity, individualism), and how its moral ambiguity chases us in every sphere of life. This famous utterance of Rimbaud is taken up with ironic and comic relish by the Czech novelist Milan Kundera in his novel *Immortality*. In the section, 'To be absolutely modern', Kundera writes: '[To] be *absolutely* modern means: never to question the content of modernity and to serve it as one serves the absolute, that is, without hesitation.'[55] Kundera has a certain political (and ideological) self-fashioning in mind, but it does have its aesthetic source and repercussion. Modernity is an amorphous norm that informs our thinking and action. We are put into a machine called modernity in a way that every sphere of our earthly existence—from life to politics, undergoes a technological transformation.

Macaulay's Curse

The idea of the nation as a metaphor of a new beast was evocatively drawn by Rabindranath Tagore. He has called the nation 'an octopus of abstractions'[56] and a 'scientific product made in the political laboratory'.[57] These two descriptions taken together fit the images proper to a sci-fi film.

What Tagore says about the nation is also true of modernity. The nation is, after all, the most defining political construct that modernity has forcibly gifted the non-Western world—thanks to colonialism. The octopus can be read as the cultural image of modernity: strange technologies that float before our vision, in our consciousness, offering us intangible spectacles whose meaning is difficult to decipher. The laboratory is a political image, where ideas are produced and unleashed upon society, like viruses. Modernity has unleashed a surplus of being.

Tagore has another striking statement that takes us to the heart of the problem of how modernity is a grand idea that paradoxically belittles its subjects:

> Man is reducing himself to his minimum, in order to be able to make amplest room for his organizations. He is deriding his human sentiments into shame because they are apt to stand in the way of his machines.[58]

The structures of modern organizations foster collective bodies that are constituted for a mechanistic purpose. People narrow their own perspective as individuals to fit themselves into the larger purpose of the collective body that constrains them. Tagore has a bleak view of modern collectivities. He thinks they constrain the possibilities of creative life and thought.

The crucial thing to note here is that, both in the case of modernity in the West as well as the modernity transported to colonies like India, the moral ambiguity of modernity works at two levels: the ambiguity within the claims and reality of modernity, and the contradictions between the egalitarian and universal principles of modernity vis-à-vis people's old loyalties towards historically established differences.

The paradox of colonial modernity is such that the idea of culture is always in question and flux, where the attempt at cultural uniqueness is fraught with utilitarian considerations. This rational instrumentality is a key feature in the condition and character of the colonized, particularly among the Indian elite and Hindus of privileged castes. It prevents them from acquiring the philosophical depth and reflectivity that modernity demands. Those who use culture as a resource to resist colonialism can't win—even as they won't lose—completely.

The political condition of colonial modernity, apart from creating a new form of rupture between communities, also created an ethical problem within a community: the absence of an overarching idea of the good, or a coherent, overarching structure of values. Since traditional norms were undergoing changes under modern political and social conditions, this problem was bound to occur.

The most glorified figure of the Enlightenment, one who is guided by secular and rational principles, eluded Indian modernity. It caused a lot of intellectual frustration, as we have noted, among secular thinkers of both the Marxist and liberal variety in India, beginning with Nehru. The expectation was misplaced. Colonized societies, Sudipta Kaviraj says, 'may not wish to emulate the West',[59] suggesting Western modernity was experienced in diverse ways. My argument is that colonized societies had no choice. They had no chance of autonomy or internal sovereignty to withstand the onslaught of Western modernity and yet could not become (for better and worse) its proper subjects.

According to Kaviraj, Tagore, Gandhi and Nehru forwarded arguments that can be called 'improvisation',[60] where changes in sociopolitical institutions and social conduct can be traditional and not Western in form, as long as they cater to reason. No amount of improvisation could free Indians from the temptation of mimicry that Macaulay knew the colonizer had successfully trapped the colonized into performing willy-nilly.

There are competing definitions of modernity itself, depending on how it is placed vis-à-vis its other frame of reference: tradition.[61] Talal Asad makes the point: 'In an important sense, tradition and modernity are not really two mutually exclusive states of a culture or society but different aspects of historicity.'[62] Modernity is a new historical condition, where tradition is no longer unmodern.

Religious traditions are historical and have developed their own relations with modernity. Liberalism and Marxism are areligious (and reason-based) traditions of thought which are also modern.

The relation between the two is summed up succinctly by Carl Schmitt who argued that 'significant concepts of the modern theory of the state are secularised theological concepts . . . where the omnipotent God turned into the omnipotent lawgiver'.[63]

This is where the distinction between tradition and modernity collapse. If there is anything distinct, it is (as Asad pointed out) *historical*. The evocation of the figure of the 'Messiah'[64] as the redeemer of the history of class conflict by Marxist thinker Walter Benjamin, or the (metaphysical) idea of the 'other'[65] in the French ethical thinker Emanuel Levinas, are all borrowed from theological concepts.

Nehru is keen that tradition metamorphoses into modernity: 'Traditions have to be . . . adapted and transformed to meet new conditions and ways of thought, and at the same time new traditions have to be built up'.[66] The 'new conditions' are the demands of modernity. It is a new time in history that announced a new mind:

The modern mind, that is to say the better type of the modern mind, is practical and pragmatic, ethical and social, altruistic and humanitarian. It is governed by a practical idealism for social betterment. The ideals which move it represent the spirit of the age, the Zeitgist, the Yugadharma. It has discarded to a large extent the philosophic approach of the ancients, their search for ultimate reality, as well as the devotionalism and mysticism of the medieval period.[67]

Nehru's idea of the 'Yugadharma' of modernity imagines a new historical ground. Tradition is reduced to a metaphor and gives way to a new social (and political) ideal. It is an integrative ideal, a combination of many values put together in the basket.

The problem persists: how does one make choices based on the most ethically persuasive idea of the good? It is clear that such choices are rarely consensual, or even possible under modern conditions of life. This problem has intrigued thinkers and writers alike.[68] Is there a way of reconcilement or redemption from this modern predicament?

We are back to the demanding nature of modernity. The problem of the modern era does not lie in the lack of reflectivity. In no other historical era have so many people become involved in reflecting on and debating the meaning of their condition. The difficulty lies in extending this culture of reflectivity to a larger number of people. It is difficult to turn the reflective demands of modernity into a popular ethic. That is why we are most often faced with insincere and shallow responses to ethical choices.

Octavio Paz in his 1966 speech, described Nehru as someone who 'belonged to a double anti-tradition'.[69] Educated at Harrow and Cambridge, Nehru developed close links with European culture and, Paz points out, 'drew inspiration from the rebellious and heterodox thought of the West'.[70] In *An Autobiography*,

Nehru describes his introduction at Cambridge to Nietzsche (who was a 'rage'[71]) and Bernard Shaw, among others. He thought of himself as 'sophisticated and talked of sex and morality in a superior way'.[72] One of Nehru's early influences, he writes, partly via Oscar Wilde and Walter Pater, was 'a vague kind of cyrenaicism'[73] (a hedonist philosophy that derived from ancient Greece of the fourth century, which considered sensual pleasure as the supreme good).

Nehru's other lineage is traced by Paz back to his ancestors who 'had frequented the Mogul court and had absorbed Persian and Arabic heritage', and to his family tradition from which 'he had a vein of heterodoxy vis-à-vis Hindu traditionalism'.[74] In the beginning of *An Autobiography*, Nehru mentions his ancestor Raj Kaul, who 'had gained eminence as a Sanskrit and Persian scholar in Kashmir',[75] catching the attention of Farrukhsiyar, the man who took over the Mughal Empire after Aurangzeb's death. Nehru's younger uncle, Nand Lal Nehru, was 'considered to be a good Persian scholar [who] knew Arabic also'.[76] A little later, Nehru mentions, '[father] and my older cousins treated the question [of religion] humorously and refused to take it seriously'.[77] When his father returned home after visiting Europe, he had to undergo the 'prayaschit' or the purification ceremony, according to Brahminical norms. But Nehru writes, he 'refused to go through any ceremony or to submit in any way . . . to a so-called purification'.[78]

Nehru emerges as a man of double modernity. This doubleness of identity across two or more cultures makes Nehru an exemplary figure. The relationship with Europe would have been modern in an intellectual but not experiential way. Nehru did not have to go through any crisis vis-à-vis Christianity. In India, however, Nehru's identity mirrored an impressive heterogeneity.

Nehru's double modernity was perhaps most responsible in making him restless towards all sorts of traditionalist tendencies.

It also made him prone to more accusations regarding his politics and sense of belonging. When conservative lawyer and politician from Madras, Sir C. P. Ramaswamy Aiyer said in public that Nehru 'did not represent mass-feeling', Nehru agreed to the verdict and extended the point in the epilogue of his autobiography:

> I often wonder if I represent anyone at all . . . I have become a queer mixture of the East and the West, out of place everywhere, at home nowhere. Perhaps my thoughts and approach to life are more akin to what is called Western than Eastern, but India clings to me, as she does to all her children, in innumerable ways . . . I cannot get rid of either that past inheritance or my recent acquisitions . . . [T]hey create in me a spiritual loneliness not only in public activities but in life itself. I am a stranger and alien in the West . . . But in my own country also, sometimes, I have an exile's feeling.[79]

The man who lived a double modernity suffered in his own admission—a sense of cultural homelessness that we may describe as spiritual *unheimlich*. The double home of East and West created a tension that was aesthetic and spiritual. To belong *and* not to belong was Nehru's cultural predicament. It produced a divided sense of self in Nehru, which is part of a larger condition of the modern self. There is an estrangement from the ascriptive modes of the self. The modern individual is thrown towards the anxious desire—in Rimbaud's words—'to be absolutely modern'.[80]

Nehru was too modern for India. Walter Crocker called him, the 'frequently un-Indian nationalist'.[81] In the beginning of *The Discovery* Nehru poses the question he seeks to find out about India: 'How does she fit into the modern world?'[82]

Nehru was already modern. India wasn't yet modern. It is not how modernity fits India, but how India fits modernity that was Nehru's concern. Modernity was the new thing. It was the new idea and sensibility that had dawned in history. India was an old idea and an old sensibility, lagging behind in time. Western modernity had announced a new time in the world, a time of radical change and progress. Modernity meant a new structure—a new apparatus of thought, life, social relations and economy.

To be modern was in India's favour. Despite being ushered in by colonial power, the spirit of modernity gave the colonized a chance to be part of universal history. It was a matter of historical inevitability. In Octavio Paz's phrase, 'the Third World is *condemned* to modernity'.[83]

Nehru's question also begged the other question that he sought to find an answer for: How do *I* as a modern subject, fit into India?

There are two aspects to Nehru's modernity and being the modern subject. One is the question of belonging. Nehru confesses:

> India was in my blood and there was much in her that instinctively thrilled me. And yet I approached her almost as an alien critic, full of dislike for the present as well as for many of the relics of the past that I saw. To some extent I came to her via the West, and looked at her as a friendly westerner might have done. I was eager and anxious to change her outlook and appearance and give her the garb of modernity.[84]

Nehru's intellectual and cultural ties with India were intercepted by another place, its history and culture. Nehru epitomized the modern traveller, who brings ideas from elsewhere. In this, Nehru was not alone. He was one among other Indian leaders and thinkers to learn and get inspired by western thought. Does that disqualify Nehru, and others like him, from belonging to India?

It is an absurd question. The territorial idea of culture is prone to absurdities. The outsider–insider question is taken to a conspiratorial level during times when nationalist politics is driven by ethnocentric sentiments. Who is less Hindu or more Hindu determines who is a good or bad Hindu[85] in ethnocentric terms. Identity is determined by a measuring tape. Less and more, in turn, is determined by who is traditionalist and who is modern. These debates often plummet to shallow polemics. It turns the question of identity, *political.*

Nehru was more than willing to tailor India for modernity. Nehru concedes modernity is a 'garb', a matter of appearance. It lacks (historical) ground, as it is still in the making. Modernity was a new and alien condition for India. Since it was rooted in traditionalist thinking and practices, India had to perform the new script of modernity. Nehru did not believe in the emulative aspect of culture and demanded genuine inspiration. It was a difficult task for a people who suffered two hundred years at the hands of a new beast called colonialism, and its colonial project of modernization. Modernity in India was destined to be a shallow act. People were reluctant to let go of their historically established social prejudices, and made ambivalent gestures towards Western values of modernity. The performance so far has been fraught with contradictions and profound shallowness. The shallow act includes Macaulay's curse of mimicking the colonizer.

India had to be dressed up to be part of the modern spectacle. The people must put up a show. Appearances are deceptive. But appearances are a mark (or sign) of reality. There may be a reality beneath the appearance, but it doesn't mean appearance doesn't have a reality of its own. Rather, appearance is caught between two realities: the reality of its appearance, and the reality of what it hides beneath it. The 'garb of modernity' is an appearance of its own reality, in the sense of its relatedness to what it is a garb of. In the *Critique of Pure Reason*, Immanuel Kant holds that the object of appearance can be construed in representational terms, as something we recognize in space and time. This appearance is not to be understood as a thing-in-itself (or how I am 'in myself'[86]).

The idea of appearance or the appearance of an idea (say, of modernity) is close, but not identical to what the idea (say, of India) is. What about the idea itself?

India is neither limited to nor exhausted by anyone's idea, including Nehru's. It is an idea that comes from the nature of one's experience. There is no escape from the fact that the experience of modernity facilitated by colonialism will play a significant part in the new idea of India. That is where the question of appearance, of Nehru's 'garb', comes into the picture. Both the idea and appearance of India fall within the problem of representation. Both idea and appearance can be deceptive, but both emerge out of a certain lived reality, which facilitates imagination. Both as idea and appearance, the question of representation is *political*. Nehru's 'garb of modernity' is an acknowledgement and desire: India is now a modern nation, and a part of universal history. The idea of progress, individual freedom, and equality are modern political virtues for Nehru, and hence a desirable part of the new idea of India.

Nehru asks himself (and us) about India quite early in *The Discovery of India*: 'How does she fit into the modern world?'[87] He is concerned about how India will face up to the challenge of modernity. Modernity was a new historical and political condition that demanded a new relationship from the people of India. Will Indian civilization fit this new historical occasion? Nehru wonders if India, like an actor suddenly called on to play his assigned role on the stage of modern history, will perform well.

The story in retrospect is that India's encounter with modernity has yielded mixed fruits. When an alien system of life like modernity is forced into a traditionalist culture, it is bound to unleash a series of paradoxes: force and resistance, enthusiasm and circumspection, acceptance and rejection. Each person at an individual level treats it differently. In this way, modernity individualizes culture. It also instrumentalizes the nature of choice. People choose more readily according to their sense of prejudice or profit. It is difficult to make a ground for the values of modernity till you integrate them with a culture. The values of a traditional culture will be at odds with the values of modernity. And we know modernity has its nasty, dark side. In Rabindranath Tagore's *Letters from Russia* (written during the poet's visit to Russia in 1930), he describes the Soviet State's overshadowing of culture in the name of collective life as the 'shadow side of the moon'.[88] Tagore saw the danger. Modernity is not the golden script of the world's deliverance from all ills. That makes the business of choice more difficult, and unenviably paradoxical. Nehru's garb of modernity is a good representation of our predicament. That garb has, however, metamorphosed beyond recognition. The story of the blue jackal in the *Panchatantra* comes to mind. It announced itself king after it had turned blue, having spent the night hiding in the washerman's tub. Modernity is a washerman's tub that produces wily creatures.

2

The Citizen and the 'Secular State Business'

The Indian republic in its seventieth year returned to political views on refugees and citizens aired by members during the Constituent Assembly Debates of 1949, as the Narendra Modi government at the Centre, passed the historic Citizenship Amendment Act (CAA) in both houses of Parliament in early December 2020. The Act introduces special provisions for Hindus, Christians, Sikhs, Parsis, Jains and Buddhists fleeing persecution in Pakistan, Afghanistan and Bangladesh.

Legal experts and scholars with secular concerns voiced their alarm against the declaration and eventual passing of the Bill in both houses of Parliament. Niraja Gopal Jayal argues that the new Act is an abrasion of the Citizenship Act of 1955, from the legal and political perspectives. Legally, Jayal explained, the Act implies 'a foundational shift in the conception of the Indian citizen' that involves 'a move from soil to blood', or 'from a *jus soli* or birth-based principle of citizenship' towards a '*jus sanguinis* or descent-based principle'.[1] Politically, the CAA involves a 'tectonic shift from a civic-national to an ethnic-national conception of the political community'.[2]

This shift involves other moments between 1955 and 2020. The 1985 Assam Accord between the Assamese students' organizations and the Rajiv Gandhi government, Jayal added, was responsible for introducing 'categories of eligibility'[3] for migrants that included a cut-off date.

In her work on citizenship, Anupama Roy points out, the Assam Accord also made a (conceptually) dubious distinction between what constitutes a citizen, and what constitutes a migrant. On the one hand, Roy argued, the Assamese people were defined in terms of 'the abstract universal citizen'.[4] On the other hand, migrants identified by their linguistic and religious identity were forced to occupy a zone of 'ambivalent citizenship',[5] where legality was suspect till proven otherwise. The migrants lived in an indeterminate (borderless) time zone, where they faced constant threat and occasional violence over their disputed status.

Almost a decade later, the 2003 Citizenship Amendment Act under the National Democratic Alliance (NDA) government introduced the category (and figure) of the 'illegal migrant'[6] in the Citizenship Act. It also prepared the contentious ground for making 'religious identity . . . the basis of legal citizenship'.[7] The political and legal precursors to the CAA show concerted moves to weaken the status of refugees or migrants, and rob them of their natural rights.

However, the shift from the 'civic' to the 'ethnic', argued by Jalal, is caught in a binary understanding. Civic nationalism is about right-bearing citizens sharing universal values like freedom and equality. Ethnic nationalism is based on cultural particularism, where the idea of belonging and solidarity is based on inherited markers of identity. If the virtues of civic nationalism are based on the individual who is presumably free and rational, ethnic nationalist claims are based on the notions of group identity.

The values of civic nationalism, however, do not fully address the problem of accommodating refugees and migrants within a nation's citizenship laws. Migrants have a collective identity, and they belong to particular communities. They move out of their national borders due to a variety of reasons: from persecution, to natural disasters, to acute issues of livelihood.

Amending the Citizenship Act of 1955, the Citizen Amendment Act (CAA) makes a partial gesture of inclusivity, but within an exclusionary framework. The idea of citizenship has been broadened to include persecuted migrants seeking asylum. The criterion includes minorities *only* from Muslim-majority countries, and persecuted Muslims have been kept out. By excluding Muslim refugees from the bill, and including everyone *except* Muslim immigrants in the proposed National Register for Citizenship (NRC), the government has closed the doors to India's largest minority from both sides.

The Debates on Citizenship

It will be illuminating at this point to draw a historical and political comparison with the mindset behind the CAA, and views expressed by certain members during the Constituent Assembly Debates of 1949. We will also find a noteworthy coincidence of how Nehru spoke of the secular State during the Constituent Assembly Debates in the context of citizenship.

On 11 August 1949 the lawyer Dr P.S. Deshmukh tabled his amendment to Article 5 of the Draft Constitution that dealt with the basic principles of citizenship in India. Deshmukh found Ambedkar's definition of anyone born within the territory of India being a citizen, 'ridiculously cheap'.[8] It is a disdainfully rude remark. Deshmukh, however, backs up his dismissal with arbitrary fancies, proving his incapacity to understand what entails an accommodating and sensitive definition of citizenship. Deshmukh found the definition lacking clarity on exemplary situations: like a child born to foreign nationals on Indian soil, or a spy who lives on for five years to execute plans of sabotage. Popular thrillers haunted the borders of his imagination.

Deshmukh was surprised to learn that there was no 'register' kept for foreigners coming to India, nor 'any rules and regulations governing the entry'[9] of such people. He was aghast that 'we should throw open our citizenship so indiscriminately'.[10]

The lack of a strict process of enumeration is understandable when the country has just achieved a painful and difficult freedom. But Deshmukh must register his territorial paranoia. Behind what he considers a reckless attitude towards strict documentation of Indian citizenship is, in his words, 'the specious, oft-repeated and nauseating principle of secularity of the State'.[11] Deshmukh elaborates his discomfort:

> I think that we are going too far in this business of secularity. Does it mean that we must wipe out our own people that we must wipe them out in order to prove our secularity that we must wipe out Hindus and Sikhs under the name of secularity, that we must undermine everything that is sacred and dear to the Indians to prove that we are secular?[12]

For Deshmukh, secularity draws a false equivalence between communities that deserve State asylum. Some communities, according to him, are more Indian than others. To deny privilege to these communities vis-à-vis minorities or others, would be undermining the 'sacred'. The secular is seen as the enemy of the sacred. The real intent of Deshmukh's inflated logic becomes clearer in the clause he wished to insert in the Article: that 'every person who is a Hindu or a Sikh and is not a citizen of any other State shall be entitled to be a citizen of India.'[13] Offering reasons behind the clause, he drew an idea of India that belonged to Hindus and Sikhs alone:

> Here we are an entire nation with a history of thousands of years and we are going to discard it, in spite of the fact that neither the Hindu nor the Sikh has any other place in the wide world to go to. By the mere fact that he is a Hindu or a Sikh, he should get Indian citizenship because it is this one circumstance that makes him disliked by others.[14]

The fact that Hindus and Sikhs can't live anywhere else in the world is an exaggeration not borne out by history. Hindus and Sikhs of considerable number have been migrating to the United States, Canada, the Caribbean islands, and parts of Europe since the nineteenth century.

Deshmukh draws upon examples from the world to showcase how Indians are 'treated all over the world'.[15] He reminds the House of the 'colour prejudice' in England, and the 'persecution' Indian nationals faced in South Africa, Malaya and Burma.[16] He also added his concerns regarding the difficulties in obtaining citizenship in America. All that Deshmukh names as clinching reasons for graded citizenship are four countries to illustrate his point. It doesn't occur to him why something that is *wrong* in certain countries should be considered the moral and political basis for India's foundational laws. Must India formulate its principles by following on the footsteps of nations that practise prejudice and persecution? Is promising equality a 'cheap' option compared to discrimination?

On 12 August 1949, Nehru took the floor to support Ambedkar's proposals and the amendment by Mr Gopalaswami

Ayyangar that all those who returned to India permanently and in possession of permanent permits shall be deemed citizens.

Nehru begins by acknowledging that Partition has created 'a very difficult and complicated situation'.[17] But he believed that whatever decision is taken must comply with 'the greatest amount of justice to our people'.[18] He conceded that there may be cases where people may not have the prerequisites of being a citizen till July 1948, the cut-off month decided for citizenship. Nehru emphasized, 'It is impossible to examine hundreds of thousands of such cases and we accept the whole lot.'[19]

It is significant to hear Nehru in the light of the political and legal quagmire brought about by the NRC in Assam. Nehru realized it wasn't practically feasible to authenticate every case of citizenship. So, it was better to allow everybody to be citizens. He was well aware of the religious prejudice prevalent in the country. He espoused 'practical commonsense'[20] in this regard. It was impossible to ascertain eligibility of citizenship for a huge number of people. Nehru wanted to avoid the legal mechanism where the fate of people seeking citizenship was in the hands of state functionaries, where the principle of fairness was sacrificed in favour of communal entitlement.

Nehru found the application of different rules for different communities 'absurd'.[21] He spoke of 'Nationalist Muslims', people who 'had absolutely no desire to go away but who were simply pushed out by circumstances' and were considered 'opponents and enemies' by people in Pakistan, who 'made their lives miserable'.[22] These Muslims, Nehru held, 'expressed a desire to come back and some of them have come back'.[23] What Nehru calls 'circumstances' were historical in nature, and evidently, catastrophic. These circumstances included fear and uncertainty. Muslims were caught in a dilemma based on fear: whether to leave for Pakistan or stay back in India. Those who faced hostility in

Pakistan and returned to India had realized their mistake. Nehru did not want their hope (in India) denied by the logic of Partition. In Nehru's secular sentiment, religion couldn't be a yardstick for belonging.

Two other members from the Debates deserve mention. Both cancelled the communal logic with an ethical use of reason and a secular sentiment that came under attack from a few members.

On 11 August, a day before Nehru had spoken, Brajeshwar Prasad—the member from Bihar, raised the question in response to a member:

> May I ask my honourable Friend whether it is true that all those persons who fled over to Pakistan did so with the intention of permanently settling down there and owing allegiance to that State? Is it not a fact that they fled in panic?[24]

Just before Nehru had taken the floor on the same day, Mr Mahboob Ali Baig Saheb, the member from Madras, reminded the House that during the transfer of power, there was an agreement by both parties to protect and safeguard minorities. He stressed the point 'that after the transfer of power there was a holocaust, there were disturbances, there were tragedies which compelled persons to migrate'.[25] Arguing against the logic of suspicion, Baig stated, 'To say those people coming to India might become traitors and therefore, they should not be allowed to come back, that is no reason at all. With this temperament you will never become strong.'[26] Muslims who left for Pakistan and came back to India acknowledged by their act the failure, and limits, of a nation imagined as a haven for a certain religious identity.

Nehru recognized the political significance of this episode. The return of these Muslims to India, more than anything else, proved the fallacy of the idea of Pakistan. By their return, these

Muslims demonstrated that Pakistan was not a good idea for all
Muslims. They were willing to abandon their apprehensions and
come back in India. The fact that they *chose* to return marks a
decisive moment of reclamation of ties.

Nehru then boldly addressed what he felt was the
indiscriminate and unfair use of the word 'appeasement' levelled
against the government:

> One word has been thrown about a lot. I should like to
> register my strong protest against that word. I want the House
> to examine the word carefully and it is that this Government
> goes in for a policy of appeasement, appeasement of Pakistan,
> appeasement of Muslims, appeasement of this and that. I want
> to know clearly what that word means. Do the honourable
> Members who talk of appeasement think that some kind
> of rule should be applied when dealing with these people
> which has nothing to do with justice or equity? I want a clear
> answer to that. If so, I would only plead for appeasement.
> This Government will not go by a hair's breadth to the right
> or to left from what they consider to be the right way of
> dealing, with the situation, justice to the individual or the
> group.[27]

The accusation of 'appeasement', Nehru saw, was political
rhetoric to ensure that the largest minority remains devoid of just
treatment and equality. The bogey of appeasement is a tactic to
divert attention from what minorities deserve in a democracy. This
expressed attitude towards minorities is the first sign of a lack of
commitment to democracy. The minorities are seen as outsiders.
Anything guaranteed to them exclusively as constitutional rights
and protection is seen as an undue favour by people with a
majoritarian mindset.

Those among the people that Nehru refers to, regarding members raising the bogey of 'appeasement', includes Seth Gobind Das. He was a parliamentarian from Jabalpur, and a close associate and follower of Gandhi.

Ambedkar presented the Draft Constitution before the House on 4 November 1948, praying the House pay attention to the issue of the protection of minorities and his advice for the 'majority to realize its duty not to discriminate against minorities'.[28] Rising in support of the motion, Das, however, put his note of difference:

> We do not want to place any minority, whether Muslim or other, under any disabilities. But, certainly we are not prepared to appease those who put the two-nation theory before us. I want to make it clear that from the cultural point of view only one culture can exist in this country. The Constitution that we adopt must be in harmony with our culture.[29]

Ambedkar may have used the term 'minority' not just for a religious minority (namely Muslims), but also the 'Depressed Classes'. Das had one minority in mind. His view prompts Nehru's outburst. Das's use of the word 'disabilities' betrays a pathological concern, and the word 'appease' determines the limit of political anxiety. Any secular gesture towards minorities is understood as generosity by Das, and Nehru finds it unacceptable. His 'we' is unabashedly majoritarian. His idea of 'one culture' is an invitation to monoculture.

Nehru next turns his attention to the misuse of the word 'secular':

> Another word is thrown up a good deal, this secular State business. May we beg with all humility those gentlemen who use this word often to consult some dictionary before

they use it? It is brought in at every conceivable step and at
every conceivable stage . . . It has a great deal of importance,
no doubt. But, it is brought in in all contexts, as if by saying
that we are a secular State we have done something amazingly
generous, given something out of our pocket to the rest of the
world, something which we ought not to have done . . . We
have only done something which every country does except a
very few misguided and backward countries in the world.[30]

*It is instructive to note here that in the making of the Indian nation
that happened in course of the Debates, Nehru brings up the question
of secularism in the context of citizenship.*

The Debates reveal that Partition had made it inevitable
for the issues of citizenship and secularism to coincide. Nation
and nationalism had become a matter of territorial-cum-cultural
sovereignty with the drawing of boundaries on religious lines.

If Pakistan was Muslim, how could India be secular? Why
should India be secular? Those who raised this ironic logic slipped
into a mode of forgetting. They weaved eulogies of India's history,
but reduced it to Pakistan—a nation without a history. They
wanted India to be a mirror image of a nation that was limited by
a religious idea and identity, a place that Salman Rushdie, in his
novel *Shame*, called, 'a failure of the imagination . . . *insufficiently
imagined*'[31]. India's problem was the opposite. It was over-
imagined, an excess of imagination.

It is evident that members taking part in the Debates wanted
an exclusionary policy of citizenship based on arbitrary examples
to argue their case. The main intention of these members was to
sideline Muslims and secure a monopoly of belonging for Hindus
and their favoured minority, the Sikhs.

In his response, Nehru lays down the first arguments for
secularism. Firstly, he cautions, don't use secularism as a holdall.

Don't put just anything in secularism's basket. Secularism is *not* a matter of generosity. Secularism is *not* appeasement. Secularism has something to do with 'justice' and 'equity'.

Since we are looking at how the idea of the secular developed closely around the concern of citizenship, let me go back to the Debates held on 8 January 1949 when Shri Algu Rai Shastri raised the question (and sought clarity on), 'Who is a citizen of India and who is not?'[32] Nehru replied to the question with a specific reference to the category of people the question affects the most: refugees. He said, 'So far as the refugees are concerned . . . we accept as citizens anybody who calls himself a citizen of India.'[33] Nehru based the idea of asylum on free will and affectivity. The decision to belong comes from the feeling to belong, and it deserves to be respected. Belonging is a decision of the heart. It is incredible that Nehru offered the right to citizenship to the people first, and not the State. Citizenship is primarily a matter of claim that people make, before it becomes a rule assigned by the State. It is not just the widest possible consideration, political or ethical, behind defining the citizen. It is also most conceivably democratic.

After Nehru's defence, Shri Alladi Krishnaswamy Iyer, a member from Madras, clarified a crucial point regarding Article 5A, which deals with cases of mass migration:

> We do not in that article make any distinction between one community and another, between one sect and another. We make a general provision that if they migrated to this country and they were born in India as defined in the earlier Constitution, then they will be entitled to the benefits of Citizenship.[34]

Even though the word 'secular' is absent, a secular and egalitarian outlook is written into the acceptance of migrants irrespective of community or sect. The *jus soli* or birth-based principle is alone valid in this case.

Speaking after Iyer, Bihar's Brajeshwar Prasad went a step further to argue:

> that the mischief of partition should not be allowed to spread beyond the *legal fact* of partition. I stand for common citizenship of all the peoples of Asia, and as a preliminary step, I want that the establishment of a common citizenship between India and Pakistan is of vital importance for the peace and progress of Asia as a whole.[35]

The communal politics of Partition, Prasad felt, must end after Independence. But it was inevitable that the logic—or the law—of that politics would linger. Partition is not just a legal but a historical fact, and it was survived by the politics that created it. On the question of migration, Prasad raised the interesting argument that everyone under the colonial territory deserved to find asylum in India. It was an anti-colonial idea of citizenship. Here was a man thinking outside the constraints of history. Prasad's suggestion of 'common citizenship' sounds like coming from another world, a sensibility that is far removed from the mindset of sacred territory, or territorial nationalism.

Prasad further said something that goes against the grain of the CAA today:

> I see no reason why a Muslim who is a citizen of this country should be deprived of his citizenship at the commencement of this Constitution, (e)specially when we are inviting Hindus who have come to India from Pakistan to become citizens of this country. People who have never been in India but have always lived in the Punjab and on the frontier have come and

become citizens of this State; why cannot a Muhammadan of
the frontier be so when we have always said that we are one?[36]

These questions tell us that the debate around the CAA is not
a new one, but a return to the inception of India's postcolonial
history. Prasad's argument is historically true. Those regions that
frontier other nations have a special political significance. These
are border states that tend to create a tension between the idea of
democracy and a nation state. Democracy is the idea where people
enjoy political rights based on citizenship. The idea of the frontier
is purely territorial. People living in the frontiers are also citizens,
but they are connected to the rest of the nation through special (or
extraordinary) laws. The source of these laws and the exceptional
status of frontiers are a colonial legacy. Elizabeth Kolsky writes:

> Colonial law on India's northwest frontier licensed what in
> other institutional contexts would have been lawless violence.
> The notion that the frontier tribes were more 'different,'
> more primitive, more backward, more unruly, enabled the
> legalization of disciplinary methods that unleashed the terror
> of empire.[37]

Colonialism managed to create a public perception in the
mainstream that people in the frontier regions are *not national
enough*. Such a perception underlies the ethnic limits of the nation
state. In his letter to Nehru, dated 7 November 1950, Sardar
Patel registers his fears and apprehension of China's expansionist
designs and includes the 'frontier' as his point of concern in these
words:

> All along the Himalayas in the north and north-east, we have
> on our side of the frontier a population ethnologically and

culturally not different from Tibetans and Mongoloids. The undefined state of the frontier and the existence on our side of a population with its affinities to Tibetans or Chinese have all the elements of potential trouble between China and ourselves.[38]

The question of national sovereignty confronts the problem of distance and unease vis-à-vis people who are seen as ethnically other, existing beyond the cultural contours of nationalist imagination. The term 'population' in this specific instance marks the ethnic nature of a people. The 'undefined state' of the frontier is undefined in relation to both law and governmentality, or the law of governmentality. The 'undefined state' of a population warrants what Giorgio Agamben calls 'the state of exception'[39]: the declaration (or undeclared presence) of an emergency law where conventional norms of the state (and government) are replaced by extrajudicial norms.

The closer the colonizer moved to the periphery, they encountered people who were geoculturally distant from the nationalist project unleashed in other parts. These peripheries were integrated through a more lawless recourse to violence. This undemocratic *imbalance* did not disappear after Independence. After 1947, the rulers changed hands but the idea of the nation remained intact. Equal citizenship laws were a gloss over historical prejudice.

In the Debates that took place on 12 August 1949, Sardar Bhopinder Singh Mann—a Sikh from East Punjab, raised the complaint that a 'weak sort of secularism'[40] has crept into the Drafting Committee's definition of citizenship. Singh objected to 19 July 1948 being kept as the cut-off date for receiving refugees from Pakistan. He argued, with a logic peppered with sarcasm, if those Hindu and Sikh refugees who wanted to escape persecution in Pakistan would have known of the prescribed date, 'they would have invited [Pakistan's] knife earlier so that they might have come here earlier and acquired citizenship rights'.[41]

Singh's apprehensions of a communal frenzy were based on the 'evacuee property talks'[42] between India and Pakistan failing on any account. His anti-minoritarian position vis-à-vis refugee settlement becomes clearer when he cites the example of the Meos, a Muslim-Rajput tribe staying around Delhi, Agra and Jaipur.[43] Singh alleged that the Meos from Gurgaon, Bharatpur and Alwar 'were involved in very serious rioting against the Hindus—their neighbours at the time of freedom', and were exploiting the 'lax permit system'[44] that allowed citizenship, apart from trading facilities to their advantage by reclaiming land. Singh thought strongly against granting 'rights of citizenship to those who so flagrantly dishonoured the integrity of India not so long ago'.[45] He believed no 'concessions'[46] can be given to such people, when property is already in short supply. 'This is secularism no doubt', Singh conceded, 'but a very one-sided and undesirable type of secularism.'[47]

Bhopinder Singh Mann's perspective on who is a legitimate refugee, who is the deserving citizen, and what is, and is not, desirable secularism, ensues from a narrative whose threads run even today. Singh exhorted Indian lawmakers to pay more attention to the fate of Hindu and Sikh refugees. His concern for minorities in Pakistan echoes Deshmukh's view that some refugees deserve more attention than others.

This is precisely the logic that the CAA is endorsing: singling out Muslims as undeserving of asylum. The secular question becomes political where it gets entangled with the question of *who* is a citizen.

To the credit of Nehru and others who thought on secular lines during the Debates, the definition of the citizen was kept porous enough for a refugee to easily fit into. Two obstacles were placed around the citizen: cut-off date and identity. Both obstacles were aired by people with a majoritarian mindset. Partition legitimized the logic that Hindus and Muslims were two divided nations.

Nehru's approach to the question of citizenship is not in any essential sort of way linked to his being secular, or his belief in secularism. His openness regarding the question of who can be an Indian citizen is based on historical sensibility.

The question of who belongs to India is a matter of historical (and natural) belonging. Someone's historical ties with a place precedes the natural. One is *naturally* born into history. The natural and the historical are adjunctive facts of identity. Anyone born in India is born into a community, and all communities in question—Hindu, Muslim, Sikh, Christian, Buddhist, and Jain—are part of India, having been part of its history.

Partition is a tragic addition to that history. It brought into play new legalities on citizenship. The idea of citizenship is based on territoriality. Belonging, as Nehru and others who thought like him understood, is a matter of feeling and sentiment. It needs to be treated with affection. Within the legal boundaries of determining citizenship, one can extend the boundaries of the heart.

Even though the problem of (granting) citizenship was not directly (or primarily) connected to secularism, the term found significant mention during the Debates. Nehru was forced to comment on secularism because some members dragged the secular word into the discussion. These members found the gesture and rationale behind accommodating refugees who returned after going over to Pakistan, as a secular compromise to accommodate the sentiments of the minorities.

The Other among Citizens

Citizenship is a legal concept, and is based on natural rights. It has a political dimension that becomes visible whenever there is a refugee or migrant issue.

During the 1979 Anti-Foreigners' Movement in Assam, people belonging to the Bengali community were put under a legal cloud. A cut-off date was demanded by Assamese leaders to identify 'foreigners', or illegal refugees from neighbouring Bangladesh, and disenfranchise them. This political demand put the legal status of all Bengalis into question. The movement to drive out 'foreigners' lasted from 1979–1985.

I witnessed and faced persecution in Assam as a schoolboy growing up in a railway colony town near Guwahati.[48] Bengalis belonging to Muslim and Hindu communities in Assam were targeted during that period in a political move to disenfranchise them, irrespective of whether they were ascertained to be citizens or not. The tag of a 'foreigner' was enough instigation for violence. The invectives in the popular slogans of the Anti-Foreigners Agitation included Nepalis and Biharis who were also considered 'outsiders'. Many commentators have written about the xenophobic tendencies of the Assam Movement.[49] In the case of Assam, language replaced religion as the basis of othering. The reasons were economic (as it always is the case): lack of resources, ownership of land and unemployment. These are transposed into the cultural sphere where minorities were marked by their language and ethnic difference. This is where an economic problem transforms into the political.

The identity of the refugee (in this case, the refugee-citizen, an absurd status of people who were citizens of India, but whose citizenship status was put under question) is a political one. Citizenship, by extension, is political.

The NRC and CAA are citizenship laws that are political in nature. Not just because of the identity of people who are marked out and whom these acts are trying to exclude. They are political in a deviously fundamental way in which they imagine certain sections of people (inevitably minorities) whose legal status is in question.

There is a legal drive to identify 'foreigners' under the NRC in Assam. The 'D Voters' (or doubtful voters) in the context of the NRC are those who don't have sufficient papers to prove their credentials of being citizens, and hence are disenfranchised. Those rendered doubtful voters have their citizenship under question. Many among them have been forced into detention centres, designed to isolate and exclude them from the world. They have been reduced to the unwanted and despised nobodies of history. They are minorities who are desperate for legal status, but their condition is political.

How does the political condition of a minority facing a challenge to their legal status as citizens, the threat of deportation, and the terrifying possibility of Statelessness, have a bearing on secularism?

Ethnic nationalisms all over the world have an anti-secular character. The term 'secular' need not be necessarily about religion alone.

Rajeev Bhargava reminds us in an essay how 'a secular state was set up in India *despite* the massacre and displacement of millions of people on ethno-religious grounds, and it has survived in a continuing context in which ethnic nationalism remains dominant throughout the world'.[50] Post-Independence, the political movements based on ethno-linguistic grounds in Assam and Maharashtra were anti-minoritarian in nature. Both were based on driving away people who were considered 'outsiders'.

In Mumbai, the Shiv Sena was behind the politics of nativism against non-Marathi speakers.[51] This was also a movement that was based on economic grounds (employment and lack of resources), but the political aspect was territorialized around linguistic identity. Just as in the case of Assam, the question was one of belonging: who were the legitimate inhabitants of the place and who weren't. The justification behind forwarding such an argument was unpretentiously majoritarian in nature.

Bhargava, in the article mentioned earlier, goes on to add that the secular State in India was 'set up to deal with the tensions continuously generated by deep religious diversity, not to offer "a final solution" by expulsion or liquidation of all but the dominant religious group'.[52] Even though 'a final solution' was certainly averted by the formation of a secular State, I would argue that a *symptom* of 'solution' remained.

Expulsion of people based on religion was avoided at a pan-India level after Partition, yet we have witnessed incidents of exodus. Many Bengalis left Assam in the aftermath of the violence that was unleashed during the Agitation of 1979–83. Migrant workers had to leave Mumbai (then Bombay) in the 1970s.

An exodus of Kashmiri Hindus or Pandits took place in January 1990, when Muslims in the Valley spearheading the insurgency movement against the Indian state targeted the Hindu minority.[53] My first encounter of the Kashmir problem was through poor, young girls from the Pandit community, who lived in the refugee camps in Delhi. They would visit our hostels in JNU, knocking on each door to collect money for sustenance. They would carry a notebook with names of donators and other details. I did not know what to ask them. I remember the lost look in their eyes. They bore their precarious condition with dignity and a heartbreaking smile. When I visited Srinagar in 2015, I realized how terrible it must have been for those little girls to leave the green shores of the river Jhelum and walk the dingy corridors of Jhelum hostel.

Was the exodus of the Kashmiri Pandits meant to be a 'solution' before the insurgency that overtook Kashmir?

There is another episode that can also be read as a 'solution' to make Jammu and Kashmir a Hindu-majority state. The massacre

of Muslims in Jammu in November 1947[54] marks the genesis of
a nationalist mindset that succumbs to brutal means in order to
balance paranoia and control. The politics of modern statecraft
that runs by calculative rationality can be brutally unethical.
Lives are sacrificed to achieve demographic balance. Because of
Partition, political power in India was seen through the prism of
communal hegemony. One community had to dominate another
politically (or Hindus had to dominate Muslims) in numerical
terms. India learnt how to achieve this logic of domination by
orchestrating massacres on the eve of its Independence.

An episode in India's political history that was kept under
wraps for decades is the 1979 massacre of the Namasudras
(outcastes of Bengali Hindu society) in Marichjhapi, an island
in the Sundarbans in West Bengal. The Jyoti Basu-led Left Front
government had come to power in 1977. The Dalit refugee
population was seeking rehabilitation, after facing persecution in
Bangladesh. Several hundred people (considered a conservative
estimate) died through starvation and unrestrained violence.
Even though the state government hasn't been indicted by any
court of law, the grievous incident served as a calculated political
'solution' to the refugee crisis in West Bengal. According to Mr
Prafulla Mandal, the Panchayat chief of Kumirmari Island, he was
asked by Basu to meet him at the Writers' Building. Basu tried to
dissuade Mandal and others with him from supporting the cause
of the refugees. When Mandal tried to sensitize the chief minister
on the plight of the refugees, he reportedly said, 'There is no place
for sentiment in politics. From now on don't cooperate with the
refugees.'[55] This statement attributed to Basu reads as a confession
of the brutal realism of communist politics.

The massacre of Muslim peasant families in Nellie can be read
as a political move to 'solve' the 'foreigners' problem in Assam. On
an ordinary morning of 18 February 1983, almost 2000 Bengali

Muslim peasant families from fourteen villages in central Assam lost their lives within six hours. They were attacked by a mix of an indigenous tribal group (the Tiwas) and Assamese Hindus.[56] In a 2015 documentary on the Nellie massacre by Subasri Krishnan, *What the Fields Remember*, two old Muslim men who lost members of their families, Sirajuddin Ahmed and Abdul Khayer, recount the day of horror. Their stories reveal they are not refugees, yet are denied proactive citizenship.[57]

The episode produced shockwaves in Delhi. The Rajiv Gandhi government at the Centre made a political deal (the Assam Accord of August 1985) with the student leaders who had spearheaded the Assam Movement since 1979.

The return of the citizenship issue in Assam has ushered in grim consequences for minorities in the state. The majoritarian shadow on the debate over citizenship is haunting India. The heated debates on citizenship that once preoccupied members of the Constituent Assembly are happening in the media, the social media and even in the streets as people protested against the NRC and the CAA.

Even though the Indian State adopted a secular approach to sort out deep religious and ethnic divide, it could not prevent region-based ethnic cleansing that was unleashed against minorities as 'solutions' to political issues. Even though the mass violence of the Orwellian year, 1984, against Sikhs in Delhi and the 2002 massacre of Muslims in Ahmedabad do not have anything to do with citizenship issues, both incidents are an open and gruesome mockery of India's secular credentials. Both 1984 and 2002 had clear political overtones and involvement. We learn how religious divisions within Indian society reflect on its (mainstream) political parties.

The other point deserving emphasis is that citizenship is not just about the legal issue of the right to belong. It also includes the sense and spirit of belonging. Citizenship guarantees formal equality to human beings in a liberal democracy. But the universal idea of citizenship is circumscribed by the politics of nationalism. People carrying a majoritarian identity (both within the nation state, as well as in the regional states dominated by linguistic majorities) often make exclusivist claims. These claims are material and political at the same time and they have to do with everything from land allocation to employment. The competitive nature of social and economic mobility adds its vicious sting to the cultural rivalries between communities. The idea of citizenship and its avowed universal values go for a toss.

The Case of Hyderabad

A test case for secularism at the advent of Independence was the merging of Nizam ruled Hyderabad, the largest princely state, with the State of India. I shall read this historic (and tragic) episode through A.G. Noorani's sensitive and scholarly work, *The Destruction of Hyderabad*. My focus will be on Nehru's approach regarding the war of accession for Hyderabad in September 1948:

> There is ample evidence that establishes that the Prime Minister of India, Jawaharlal Nehru, was as against it [an armed attack—'disingenuously called a 'police action'—by India against the Nizam] as the Deputy Prime Minister, Vallabhbhai Patel, was determined on this ruinous course. Their disagreement reflected a wider divide. Patel did not share Nehru's vision of a secular India, nor his attitude towards Muslims of India.[58]

Noorani suggests that a secular sensibility is expected to care for people belonging to other communities. Secularity must adhere to an ethics that questions the logic and machination of territoriality, or territorial nationalism, on the basis on religion or ethnicity. Being secular is an ethical 'attitude' towards others who are different by ethnicity, race, religion and gender.

Nations whitewash uncomfortable facts of their history. They perform an original act of forgetting in order to institute the official record of memory.

Noorani observes, 'Nehru's attitude on war was characteristically ambivalent. He did not disclaim the military operation. Far from it, but he recoiled from its consequences.'[59] He quotes Nehru, who said at a civic reception in Ooty on 2 June 1948: 'We do not propose to make Hyderabad accede by coercion. We may be compelled to it if the situation is such as to *imperil our security*.'[60]

The stated reason behind India's military operation was cited as 'law and order' that Noorani rightly finds qualitatively and 'fundamentally different'.[61] The difference is obvious: law and order is a matter internal to the State (in this case, Hyderabad), whereas security is a territorial matter between two sovereign States (in this case, between Hyderabad and India). There is a sleight-of-hand technique at play, where different reasons were offered by India as grounds for the assault on Hyderabad. The claims of territorial nationalism are dubious as it knows it transgresses ethics and wants to hide it and keep it off the records.

There is also a problem with the argument of modern statism being a superior form of political system, particularly when it aids the justification of a new territoriality. In a letter dated 15 April 1948, Nehru wrote, 'Our position has been and is that the people of Hyderabad cannot continue to live under an authoritarian and feudal regime.'[62] He called Hyderabad a 'feudal island in democratic India'.[63]

To use the 'backward' status of a political regime as the logic of annexation is to accept war as a legitimate means to establish a democratic State. If a postcolonial nation makes the argument that establishing democracy by the use of force is justified, it slips into a colonial logic. Such are the damaging ironies of colonial modernity.

Nehru wrote in the same letter, dated 3 August 1948:

> There is no instance in history so far as I am aware, when a land-locked territory, surrounded on all sides by one State, has become independent. Both in strict law, and in fact, the notion of Hyderabad's independence is a little absurd.[64]

Nehru forwards the argument that the political fate of a place depends—by a fact of nature and law—on its territorial status.

Noorani keeps coming back to the difference between Nehru and Patel:

> Their differences [Nehru and Patel's] were fundamental and stemmed from their different conceptions of what India should be. Nehru was not against the military option in principle, he supported it only as last resort. For Patel, it was the first resort. He had no patience with talks. Nehru had contempt for the Nizam's set-up but bore no malice towards him personally. He regarded Hyderabad's culture which friends like Sarojini Naidu epitomized. Patel hated the Nizam personally and ideologically opposed Hyderabad's composite culture. Nehru's concern was to avert India's balkanization by defeating Hyderabad's secessionist venture . . . Nehru was an ardent Indian nationalist. On both States, Vallabhbhai Patel was a strident Hindu nationalist.[65]

Noorani's wants to retain a qualitative distinction between 'Indian nationalist' and 'Hindu nationalist'. There is a need to complicate that distinction beyond what makes the former inclusivist and the latter, exclusivist. Both are complicit when it comes to taking hard, realist decisions that involve staking claims of sovereignty at the cost of human lives. If we consider the territorial concerns regarding the invasion of Hyderabad, the Nehru–Patel distinction doesn't hold beyond a point. Both are constrained by a certain logic that is historically enforced upon them by colonialism. The nation-state is constructed around (the idea of) borders. Borders are a rational necessity and yet paradoxically, they mark the nation's paranoia.

It is on the question of borders that reason succumbs to madness. In other words, madness (and the madness of nations) thrives on the borders of reason. The problem with all forms of nationalism is its identitarian nature. When you are challenged in racist, religious, ethnic, casteist or gendered terms, there is an ethical potential in the response against the power that challenges your identity. In other words, when an identity is made *other*, a politics of resistance and affirmation in identitarian terms is ethical. Identity *in itself* is not. This distinction is crucial to distinguish between the ills of identity that we encounter through the prejudice and violence of majoritarianism, and the promise of identity that occupies the stage of history through politically challenged minorities. The ethical promise of identity in history is in most cases, minoritarian.

We accept the political idea of nationalism that is in conflict with (colonial) power. It is necessary to challenge a foreign power that has robbed people of their sovereignty by force. Hence, a nationalist movement that seeks to overthrow that unjust power is legitimate. If this logic is extended to cater to a sentiment where you want to throw out or eliminate *other people* living alongside you, who belong to different linguistic and religious communities (or even national communities, for instance the 'foreigner' tag against Sonia Gandhi), then we have a nationalist argument that is ethnic and xenophobic in nature.

Nehru's nationalism, in this comparative sense, tempers the problem during the invasion of Hyderabad. He was careful in his instructions. He wanted the military to move in cautiously so as to inflict minimum harm on the people.[66] One can see in the letter to his Defence Minister, Baldev Singh (see endnotes), Nehru was sensitive to the minor details of the military's advancement into Hyderabad because his major concern was to avoid a human crisis. Force was meant to be used *in the last instance.*

Noorani brings the question back to Nehru's democratic secularity: 'Nehru loathed the Nizam's rule, but admired Hyderabad's non-communal, composite culture, his last-minute hesitation was prompted by an awareness it would destroy that culture and invite revenge on Muslims.'[67]

Noorani makes a distinction between the political and the cultural. Nehru's political motivation to end the Nizam's rule is distinct from his love for Hyderabadi culture and his concern for its people. Nehru's secularity stems from his cultural sensibility. The fact that cultural sensibility influences secularity has a bearing on the question of identity.

There has been a return to the politics of identity in recent times, and this has given place to contentious debates around the issue. The debates often involve the question of the citizen, as well as around the problem of majoritarianism and challenges faced by minorities. The accommodative constraints of a liberal and universal idea of secular identity appear vis-à-vis people with a *political* identity.

I Is Not Identity

The term 'identity politics' or politics of identity, involves ascriptive identities that face and challenge all forms of discrimination by people belonging to a dominant identity (of religion, race, ethnicity, caste or gender). These dominant identities impose majoritarian forms (and norms) of power. Identity politics is also a politics of (shared) experience where a whole group of people belonging to a particular religion, caste or gender identifies itself with structures of oppression and discrimination. Identity politics is not just a politics of affirmation that is produced by majoritarian resurgence too. It is a *response* (and challenge) against the hegemonic tendencies of dominant groups. The ethics of identity politics is its response and challenge to power.

Identity politics is the politics of the *other*. Blacks, Red Indians, underprivileged castes, Dalits and Jews have been historically othered. Muslims (often, specifically as Palestinians and Kashmiris) have been othered in the West soon after the birth of Israel, and in India since Independence (both moments occurring around the mid-1940s).

Refugees or migrants (Bengalis in Assam, Rohingyas in Myanmar, Mexicans in America) are also at the mercy of State laws and xenophobia. They are also identities that are othered and face persecution. Because their legal status and their right to belong are put on hold, they are incapable of identity politics.

Politics needs a real *ground*. Refugees and migrants lack that ground. They are beleaguered identities that affirm by their presence the denial of their legal, humanitarian and political status. This denial and counter-affirmation is integral to political and ethical exploration of what is identity. But what is it? What is the nature of identity? The term is much debated with proponents describing its positive content, and critics arguing its limitations and problems. Let me propose (and provoke) a negative affirmation, to highlight the antinomian nature of identity:

Identity is not identical to itself.

In other words, we are not identical to our identity. Every identity is a secret: of being a bit other to itself. Arthur Rimbaud famously declared in a letter written in 1871 to his friend and minor poet Paul Demeny—'I is another'.[68] Rimbaud suggests that I is not what it is. I is otherwise. If I may extend the proposition: *I is not identity. I is not identical to itself.*[69]

I is/am another—both as experience and possibility. You can't fully claim to be just one thing, and not the other thing. Identity is not a definition, but a tendency.

The politics of identity involves presence, or visibility. People show their face to assert their difference. Identity is singular and cannot be subsumed into a totality. A totality involves a majority that speaks in religious, ethnic, racist, casteist and gendered terms. Identity politics by historical (and political) design, therefore, always involves minorities. For this reason, you may also call it the politics of the 'minor'. The term 'minor'–being 'minor' or being a minority—isn't just about identity, but a condition (and a relation) you live under. The religious, ethnic, and sexual minority is conditioned by numbers and circumstance. They are people who are supposed to follow norms set by the majority.

Since identity is not identical to itself, it is also not identical to totality. That is why identity politics breaks the norm of (majoritarian) consensus.

Take the issue of liberal secularity when it involves political symbols and language that are deployed in the public sphere.

During the anti-CAA protest movement, there was a clear liberal discomfort regarding Muslims chanting slogans like 'Allah Hu Akbar' (God is great) and 'La ilahaillallah' (there is no God but Allah). The Congress politician and writer Shashi Tharoor tweeted that such slogans showcase a problem of 'identity politics' and 'Muslim communalism'.[70]

This is an old problem of the liberals that takes us back to the anti-colonial period. Tracing the genealogy of the term 'communalism' (and 'communal'), Shabnam Tejani writes, 'In the two decades before 1947 . . . communalism was the term that stood in for the politics of religious minorities, especially that of the Muslim minority.'[71] Any 'public presence of religion'[72] was deemed communal.

In his reflections on the issue of "States and Minorities", published in early 1947, Ambedkar corroborates Tejani's point:

Indian Nationalism has developed a new doctrine which may be called the Divine Right of the Majority to rule the minorities according to the wishes of the majority. Any claim for the sharing of power by the minority is called communalism while the monopolizing of the whole power by the majority is called Nationalism.[73]

Political rights demanded by minorities is dubbed communal from two anxieties, one being the liberal anxiety against identity-based claims, which often fuses surreptitiously with a majoritarian reluctance to share power, something that Ambedkar is clearly suggesting. Mainstream nationalists during the anticolonial movement seemed to believe that if a minority asserts a political identity it can only be to the detriment of the nation. Mainstream nationalists during the anti-colonial movement seemed to believe that if a minority asserts a political identity, it can only be to the detriment of the nation. Tharoor is pandering to a similar belief.

The politics of the Muslim League that led to Partition and the creation of Pakistan cemented the view in Independent India that minority politics is detrimentally divisive. It was on 23 March 1940 that Muhammad Ali Jinnah, the leader of the League, 'called on Indian Muslims to adopt the demand for the "independent states of Pakistan" at the League's session in Lahore'.[74] Till then, there were negotiable opportunities that were lost. The crucial occasion was setting up of the Nehru Committee in 1928, under the chairmanship of Motilal Nehru, to draft a constitution. The central issue (or hurdle) was to solve the 'communal question'[75] that primarily involved Muslims. The Nehru report opposed Jinnah's proposal of granting proportional representation in Muslim majority provinces (in lieu of giving up the demand for separate electorates).[76] The negotiations deteriorated from there, and so did Jinnah's intransigence.

The important question to ask is: Why did the leaders of the Congress, the Muslim League, the Hindu Mahasabha and others allow the precipitation of political differences to endanger the lives of millions? Because in politics, let it be said as harshly as possible, the lives of ordinary people do not matter.

The current Bharatiya Janata Party (BJP) regime has pushed the debate back to Partition. The Hindu right, formed on the basis of anti-minority sentiments, cannot imagine beyond what it lost (and found) in Partition. The tragic paradox of the Hindu right is that it does not accept the logic of Partition, and yet its politics is fuelled by the success of that logic.

Indian liberals, including Congressmen like Tharoor, are stuck in the secularist language of the anti-colonial period. Even though liberal secularists will define secularism in relation to religion, *politically* the idea of the secular is always sought to be rescued from its opposite: communalism.[77] For these liberals, identity politics *is* narrowly communal by definition and design. This unthinking position leads to a poor and narrow understanding of how a minority is expected to respond to a political crisis that affects the community. To pigeonhole the response of a minority community against abrasive majoritarianism, where it must maintain a language perceived (and judged) as either communal or national, is to erect a communal/national binary. It has an anti-minoritarian streak (since the late 1920s) that can be termed *secular majoritarianism.*

Shifting back to 2019, when Muslims protested in the streets against the CAA—a student of Aligarh Muslim University (AMU), Hayaat Fatemah, argued in The *Indian Express*, this is 'not the right time' for a 'Muslim empowerment movement'[78] against Islamophobia, and that religious sloganeering may lead to further othering.

There is never a right time (there is always a right time) to counter historical prejudice.

In Fatemah's understanding, 'the citizenship of a Muslim is questioned, not his religious identity'.[79] That is not an accurate observation.

It is on the basis of their religious identity alone that the citizenship rights of Muslims are being compromised. Fatemah draws a spurious binary between identity and citizenship. In the Debates of 1948, nationalist lines were drawn by certain members between Muslims and Indian citizenship. There were arguments questioning Muslims regarding their natural ties with India. Liberals like Nehru rose to defend the right to citizenship of Muslims on the basis of equality, justice and belonging. Nehru also mentioned 'Nationalist Muslims' who are attached to India by sentiment.

It was perhaps not the best moment to discuss what makes Muslims nationalists, and what the source of their sentiment is. It can, however, be asked today: Does the inclination to be a secular citizen (especially for the minority) mean hiding their religious identity in public? Is being Muslim in public a danger to the Hindu? Is the Hindu–Muslim relationship to be viewed only through the lens of secular citizenry, where being both secular *and* citizen must mean an erasure of Hindu-ness and Muslim-ness?

Being Muslim or Hindu by faith or religion is an inescapable (if not essential) part of identity. Identity is political and nonpolitical, depending on circumstances.

The liberal prejudice is that there is something wrong in a minority that indulges in identity politics. The minority is often compelled to respond to majoritarian politics that is based on the othering of (minority) identity. Identity politics, as discussed above, is a politics to protect the rights and dignity of identity that is under threat. A code is being enforced where the (political) presence of Muslims is being systematically erased. Muslims know that and want to reassert their presence as a community. If feeling victimized as a Muslim needs to be couched in liberal-humanist language, it discounts the voice of real diversity.

Secular Indians do not serve secularism by shying away from acknowledging what *Muslims suffer as Muslims*.

The banality in the liberal argument lies in the unrecognized contradiction of their language: If you stand for real diversity, you must (at least, logically) stand for what grants real, demonstrative meaning to that diversity. *If* Muslims suffered as (liberal) individuals, they can surely protest the same way. What if that is not the case?

Tharoor writes in his tweet, the 'issue is about constitutional values, the foundational pluralist idea of India'.[80] Muslims have raised religious slogans, displayed their cultural identity, as well as read out the Preamble of the Constitution with fellow Hindus while protesting against the CAA.[81] Even at the performative level, there is an assertion of the *simultaneity of identity*, of being both Muslim and citizen.

Civil rights activist Javed Anand pointed out that Muslims were protesting not because they felt their 'deen' (or faith) was in danger, but because they had to defend their 'dastoor' (or

Constitution), as their citizenship was in danger.[82] The assertion of identity has remained *alongside*—not in contradiction to, or in conflict with—the commitment towards the constitution. It was a gesture of the Muslim citizen.

Tharoor also makes this fuzzy point in the same tweet: 'We will not allow pluralism & diversity to be supplanted by any kind of religious fundamentalism.'

These are unexamined, hyperbolic and spurious distinctions made by liberals who want the meaning of diversity to remain only in the cultural sphere. They feel alarmed the moment there is any *political* content to the meaning of identity.

Liberal secularists evoke pluralism and diversity as content-empty terms and use them to critique any political assertion on the basis of religious/cultural identity. Culture, fostering the diversity that Indian liberals love to flaunt, is not just an artefact to be paraded at Rajpath during Republic Day. It has a political meaning and existence *outside* what culture serves on the platter of liberal democracy.

During the anti-CAA protests, Hindus and Muslims learnt about each other through immense proximity during a political movement. No knowledge (of pluralism, diversity, difference) can offer better clues about each other than real proximity. Such an experience alone can promise and produce social intimacy. A solidarity that cuts through the manufactured politics of enmity is also political. Liberals need to put their political stakes in *real* (and not imagined) diversity.

In tracing the issue of minority politics and 'communalism' in India across the decades (1928–2019), Nehru's views may help in understanding the roots of the liberal secularist discomfort regarding the politics of identity. Is identity antithetical to secularism?

Fear of Numbers

In the section titled 'The Question of Minorities' in *The Discovery of India*, Nehru offers his explanation on the rise of Muslim politics and Jinnah. He writes:

> The communal problem, as it was called, was one of adjusting the claims of the minorities and giving them sufficient protection from majority action . . . Latterly religion, in any real sense off the word, has played little part in Indian politics, though the word is often used and exploited . . . In political matters, religion has been replaced by what is called communalism, a narrow group mentality basing itself on a religious community but in reality concerned with political power and patronage.[83]

By Nehru's distinction, communalism is not about religion, but a politics of negotiation based on religious identity, or what is today known as, identity politics. He was fine about 'basic constitutional provisions'[84] that ensured protection of cultural and fundamental rights. Beyond that, Nehru felt, more demands made on the State by the minority community borders on paranoia: 'What remained? Fear that bigger numbers might politically overwhelm a minority.'[85] The fear bothering the Muslims, Nehru suggests, is the fear of big numbers. Nehru thinks the 'numbers' responsible for minority paranoia, come from a specific class of people comprising the 'peasantry and the workers'.[86] They comprise, Nehru thinks, 'the masses of all religious faiths'.[87] The idea of the 'mass' cannot rest on stable social groups belonging to any class. The mass is also an urban phenomenon. It occupies a political space where various social groups converge. Nehru, however, believes that the fear that stalks the minority is not real, but manufactured:

[P]eople had grown so accustomed to think along lines of religious cleavage, and were continually being encouraged to do so by communal religious organizations and Government action, that the fear of the major religious community, that is the Hindus, swamping others continued to exercise the minds of many Moslems.[88]

Communal organizations may well be prone to spreading misinformation, lies and paranoia. They need not belong to a minority community alone.

I mentioned the old man who worked for a Hindu organization and visited our home in Assam during weekends to deliver pamphlets to Baba. He often broke into gruesome stories of Partition without invitation. The man never condemned the violence. Instead, he exacerbated its communal nature in our minds. The motive was to keep the fear and hatred of the enemy alive. He was doing his political duty.

Nehru would have known that the propaganda machinery of minority phobia runs deep into India's history. In contrast to Nehru's concern about the fear of 'bigger numbers', the reverse phenomenon that has stalked the birth and political lives of the nation state and caused much damage to its history is what Arjun Appadurai calls the 'fear of small numbers':

Numerical majorities can become predatory and ethnocidal with regard to *small numbers* precisely when some minorities (and their small numbers) remind these majorities of the small gap which lies between their condition as majorities and the horizon of an unsullied national whole, a pure and untainted national ethnos.[89]

The many instances of mass violence as a mode of 'solution' in Independent India corroborates with Appadurai's insight. It is well known where the real fear was coming from and against whom it was directed. It is the fear of the majority against the minority, the fear of the 'bigger numbers' against 'small numbers'. The possibility that the fear of the minority against majoritarianism may be real doesn't occur to Nehru during the time (1942–45) he is writing the book.

Nehru thinks State protection and political representation are enough (rational) measures against fear. He believes, 'fear is not reasonable'.[90] Of course, fear isn't assuaged by reason. That doesn't make fear less real, or less believable. Nehru's rationalist understanding of fear does not suspect that modern politics creates rational structures of power that do not address people's fears. Whether these fears are real or imaginary is not the issue. Fear is irrational and unreasonable. It is necessary to understand the nature of rationalist politics (and power) that produces what it fails to curb: fear.

Nehru's failure to take minoritarian fear seriously makes him vulnerable to the criticism against secular majoritarianism.

It comes from a source that is evident in his language. He pointed out the limits and complications of representation (and protection) in cases where Muslims were in a majority or in equal number as Hindus and Sikhs. The underlying principle behind Nehru's discomfort towards offering special provisions to the Muslim minority was based on the idea of nationalist imagination:

It was obvious that even for purely political reasons the Congress was eager and anxious to bring about a communal solution and thus remove a barrier to progress. There was no such eagerness in the communal organizations, for their chief reason for existence was to emphasize the particular demands of their respective groups, and this had led to a certain vested interest in the *status quo* . . . [O]n two fundamental questions the Congress stood firm: national unity and democracy.[91]

The 'communal solution' granting special provisions at the level of representation (of power) and protection (of life and interests) was meant to remove a *barrier to progress*. Minority rights were communal in nature and were a hindrance to both unity and democracy. The power of the majority must be limited, but that is the only power that unites and makes the nation one. The minority breaks the idea of national unity into two. Even after Independence, speaking in the Constituent Assembly in 1948, Nehru highlights the problem of communalism as a specific problem posed by the minority: '[A] minority in an independent State which seeks to isolate and separate itself does some injury to the cause of the country.'[92] A minority, Nehru felt, has the *political* tendency to create division. He thought national unity in all respects was possible only through political oneness. It did not occur to him that oneness is premised upon (and requires) twoness. Unity is a paradox. The articulation of difference is *not necessarily* a political threat to the oneness, or unity, of the nation. Twoness introduces our inevitable and perpetual condition of (and tension between) conflict and reconciliation.

When Mr B.G. Kher argued with Ambedkar that he can't hold that the depressed classes have 'precedence' over the country as 'the part can never be greater than the whole', the latter replied, 'I am not a part of the whole; I am a part apart.'[93] Ambedkar makes the point brilliantly that if the significance of the whole lies in being whole, the significance of the part lies in being a/part. The subtractive is as crucial for the whole as the additive. It is only through twoness that oneness is established.

Something similar was echoed by Muhammad Iqbal who writes in 1944:

I can say with perfect confidence that the Muslism of India
will not submit to any kind of political idealism which would
seek to annihilate their cultural identity. Sure of this they may
be trusted to know how to reconcile the claims of religion and
patriotism.[94]

This statement does not pit identitarian sensibilities against secular
idealism. Muslims do not have to lose their Muslim-ness to be
good citizens. Iqbal suggests simultaneity of belonging rather than a
division between identity and politics. It can help us think beyond
the public-private dichotomy. The key word Iqbal uses is 'trusted'.

Nehru believes the articulation of identity by a minority in the
political sphere goes against the feeling of oneness. The minority
disturbs its affective ties with the nation by reaffirming its twoness.
Difference is understood as separateness. It is not given a thought
that perhaps the minority is not seeking to disturb its ties with
the nation, but it is the nation that imposes a certain necessity in
a minority to emphasize its concerns and boundaries. The view
that the totality of the national community cannot be challenged
by the singularity of minority identity betrays two majoritarian
concerns: That there is need for a uniformity of rights within the
nation state (a 'uniform civil code'). And secondly, any political
demand made by the minority qua minority necessarily stems
from a divisive sentiment.

The politics of unity, of oneness, is always haunted by what
splits it into two.

It is relevant to our discussion to briefly contrast at this point
how Ambedkar understood the minority in political and ethical
terms in relation to Nehru.

Partha Chatterjee explains Ambedkar's position in his lucidly
argued essay, 'Ambedkar's Theory of Minority Rights'. Chatterjee

quotes Ambedkar's statement on behalf of the Bahishkrit Hitakarini Sabha (or the Depressed Classes Institute of then Bombay) before the Indian Statutory Commission, a team of British Parliamentarians that visited India in 1928:

> I do not quite accept the principle of representation of minorities according to population in the legislature as though it were a museum of so many communities. A Legislative Council is more than a museum, it is a place where, for instance, social battles have to be fought, privileges have to be destroyed, and rights have to be won.[95]

Though Ambedkar here is primarily speaking for the Depressed Classes (a term used for Dalits in official terminology), it is part of what Chatterjee considers Ambedkar's 'general theory of minority rights'[96] meant for minorities including Muslims. The wider import of Ambedkar's point here is: one, the principle of designating minoritarian identity in a democracy must not rest only on the crude criteria of mere numbers or population. And two, the political identity of a minority involves battles for rights against majoritarian (and hierarchical) privileges.

Ambedkar had a dynamic view of minority identity. Nehru's static idea of minority representation was focused on complexities based on numerical imbalances between majority and minority populations, in spatial (or, geographical) terms within the nation state alone. Ambedkar had a marked difference with Nehru's protectionist attitude towards minorities and his liberal discomfort towards a political minority, or a minority that seeks political rights (of representation, special privileges, etc.). Ambedkar had explicitly stated what makes a minority deserve political representation: 'A minority which is oppressed, or whose rights are denied by the majority, would be a minority that would be fit for consideration for political purposes.'[97]

Unlike Nehru, Ambedkar welcomes the political agency of the minority. Ambedkar affirms minoritarian politics as a legitimate response to majoritarian hegemony. The communal nature of minority rights was not 'communalism' for Ambedkar, a blanket term Nehru used for all communities asking for special rights.

Chatterjee adds in this regard that Ambedkar 'does not make any significant attempt, like liberal political theorists, to reconcile a conception of minority rights with individual freedom and equality'.[98] Ambedkar adheres to the idea of what Chatterjee calls a 'collective autonomy and the will to self-representation'[99] of the minority.

This autonomy is granted a parallel *political* legitimacy alongside the rights of the individual. Nehru, in contrast, understood the guaranteeing of refugee rights as well as minority protection from the perspective of a liberal democrat, where equality and the relative freedom of the individual are the main concerns. What mattered for Nehru is the 'adjustment of the relations between individuals and between groups, of a continuous becoming something better and higher of social development'.[100]

It is the social progressivist perspective of the *becoming* of individuals and groups alike. The fate of 'democratic liberalism'— an idea that emerged in Europe since the nineteenth century— was undergoing a change after the war, which Nehru believed was moving towards a new reconciliation:

> The importance of the group and the community is emphasized more now, and the problem is to *reconcile* the respective claims of the individual and the group. The solution of that problem may take different forms in different countries, yet there will

be an ever-increasing tendency for *one basic solution* to apply to all.[101]

Nehru held on to the prospect of 'one basic solution', but he acknowledged the growing relevance of community rights.

It is necessary to offer a twist in this comparison between Ambedkar and Nehru when it concerns the case of the Muslim minority.

Shabnum Tejani observed a 'deep ambivalence'[102] in Ambedkar's view of the Muslim question. She mentions how Ambedkar recognized the Muslim demand for Separate Electorates in 1906, from where he drew out his own arguments for Separate Electorates for Dalits. In *Pakistan or the Partition of India*, even though Ambedkar agreed that Hindus and Muslims have a commonality of 'shared cultures',[103] he insisted that they were separated by a 'common historical memory'[104] and by sentiments or emotions, and a 'different destiny'.[105] Ambedkar's belief that Muslims cannot owe 'allegiance'[106] to India—despite him 'carefully considering the future of the Muslim minority in India'—comes from what Tejani calls, 'his deep resistance to Islam.[107]

Ambedkar picks up the popular trope about Muslims in *Pakistan*. He writes: 'The brotherhood of Islam is not the universal brotherhood of man. It is brotherhood of Muslims for Muslims only': hence, it 'can never allow a true Muslim to adopt India as his motherland and regard a Hindu as his kith and kin'.[108] If Muslims are solely loyal to the idea of pan-Islamism, then their cause of minority rights that Ambedkar credits them for can appear to be instrumentalist and mere self-preserving. I would read Ambedkar's ambivalence in terms of how he looks at the real stakes of Muslims as a minority community *differently* from his view of political Islam in India.

Nehru understands the impact of Islam in India and of Indian Muslims as a flowering (and deepening) of a cultural identity that is unique. He writes in *The Discovery*, 'An Indian Christian is looked upon as an Indian wherever he may go. An Indian Moslem is considered an Indian in Turkey or Arabia or Iran, or any other country where Islam is the dominant religion.'[109] One may ask: How vague or concrete is this Indianness of the Indian Muslim? One of the answers Nehru provides is:

> The fierce monotheism of Islam influenced Hinduism and the vague pantheistic attitude of the Hindu had its effect on the Indian Moslem. Most of these Indian Moslems were converts bred up in and surrounded by the old traditions; only a comparatively small number of them had come from outside.[110]

Ambedkar speaks of 'incomplete conversions' and finds it a 'mechanical cause'[111] behind the common characteristics between Hindus and Muslims. His reading of Ernest Renan, on what makes a nation, made Ambedkar conclude something quite different:

> In depending upon certain common features of Hindu and Mahomedan social life, in relying upon common language, common race and common country, the Hindu is mistaking what is accidental and superficial for what is essential and fundamental. The political and religious antagonisms divide the Hindus and the Musalmans far more deeply than the so-called common things are able to bind them together.[112]

Is Nehru's historical understanding regarding the deeply layered identities of the Hindu and the Muslim superficial?

The problem with Ambedkar's historical judgement is that it weighs too much on the politics of nationalism (what he calls 'political'). Once the idea or claim of nationalism gets divided on religious lines, the truth of history doesn't matter very much. Ambedkar is arguing on the basis of the Muslim League's reading of India's history and its Muslims. The League is more interested in carving out a distinct political cause rather than establishing historical nuances.

Ambedkar, however, gives the stern reminder that '[whether] the minority is a community or a nation, it is a minority and the safeguards for the protection of a minor nation cannot be very different from the safeguards necessary for the protection of a minor community'.[113] The necessity is facilitated by what Ambedkar calls—borrowing the phrase used in various ways by Western political thinkers from Alexis de Tocqueville to John Stuart Mill—the 'tyranny of the majority'.[114] If a community, be it a potential nation or only a minority, has a 'minor' status, it must be protected from majoritarian power. Ambedkar's argument that the 'minor' in any form—community or nation—holds the right to safeguard its identity is a politically ethical one. His political sociology, or his exaggerated reasons behind Muslims being another nation, remains contentious.

Nehru's historical point may be less political but no less real for the lack of it.

A political point of difference between Nehru and Ambedkar is that Ambedkar, despite his problem in recognizing the Indianness of Islam, backed the Muslims on the question of minority rights. Nehru, who was more welcoming of the Indian variety of Islamic faith, was uncomfortable granting Muslims the status of politically vibrant minority. This difference was due to Ambedkar's willingness in granting political autonomy to the community, which Nehru was against.

In his letter to the chief ministers on 20 September 1953, Nehru wrote:

[A] more insidious form of nationalism is the narrowness of mind that it develops within a country, when a majority thinks itself as the entire nation and in its attempt to absorb the minority actually separates even more. We in India, have to be particularly careful of this because of our tradition of caste and separatism. We have a tendency to fall into separate groups and to forget the larger unity.[115]

This is a perfect instance to understand the roots of Nehru's ambivalence. He realizes how majoritarianism poses a threat to a diverse and secular nation by its mono-cultural project. The politics of sameness intensifies separation. In the desire for a 'larger unity', the reality of twoness is not just emphasized but found undesirable.

Paradoxes of Identity

The Spanish poet Antonio Machado put this ethical predicament with brilliant precision and lucidity:

> The *other* does not exist: this is rational faith, the incurable belief of human reason. Identity=Reality, as if, in the end, everything must necessarily and absolutely be *one and the same.* But the other refuses to disappear; it subsists, it persists, it is the hard bone on which reason breaks its teeth.[116]

Machado's ethical self is *not* identitarian. The self-awareness of identity is that it is 'another' (Rimbaud). By being another, self-identity resists being both (reduced to) itself and (obliterated by) totality. The other that Machado speaks of is not just the (concrete) other out there in the world, but also the otherness within. We are all a little other to ourselves. Ethical self-identity is not subsumed by one's ethnic or religious association, or by one's nationality. But—and this is the crucial point—for ethical self-identity to exist (in its otherness to itself and the world), identity as a singular resistance against totality must exist in the first place. This totality, however, can be the ethnicity, religion or nation that you are a part of. To be an ethical self-identity, and resist totality in all forms, one must be (and become) *minor*.

The disease of majoritarianism is to be against those who break the fantasy of being one (and the same). Majoritarianism is identity that identifies itself completely with totality. The violence unleashed by majoritarianism is always partly directed against itself, for the minor is always within (its idea, its space, and its lived reality). Even the Muslim, the Dalit and the refugee can be trapped by a majoritarian understanding of itself and owing allegiance to a totality. Both liberal individuality and a Marxist idea of class can subsume the idea of the minor into *one* nationalist identity. Both individual and class are universalizable realities (and categories) of belonging and identification. Identity is *not* universal.

Identity also creates paradoxes. Nehru's own identity was no exception.

Nehru was a man of the Enlightenment, a believer of 'the scientific temper'[117] that he associated with 'the temper of a free man'.[118] The fusion of these two ideas was behind Nehru's idea of progress and democracy. The free man is the free individual, free from communal (or identitarian) bonds. Nehru was clearly not fond of particularism ('particular demands of . . . respective groups'). The free individual is free of identity, a believer of science and (social and economic) progress.

For Nehru, the minor was a major problem. He was obsessed with totality, in the name of unity (majority) and democracy (a system that fosters individuals). The problem of nationalism is that it makes itself available to totality in some form or the other. Nehru was a liberal who was anti-majoritarian in the religious and ethnic sense. Yet he is unable to shrug himself off from the logic that lends itself to secular majoritarianism. This problem cannot be understood by Marxist and liberal scholars stuck on class and individual as the fundamental reality of self-identity. Both subsume otherness.

To draw a closure on the question of identity, I shall discuss how Nehru imagines and constructs his own identity.

In *An Autobiography*, Nehru writes:

I was accused by some leaders of the Hindu Mahasabha of my ignorance of Hindu sentiments because of my defective education and general background of 'Persian' culture. What culture I possess, or whether I possess any at all, is a little difficult for me to say.[119]

For the Mahasabha, the genealogy of Nehru's proximity to Persian culture was reason to disqualify his Hindu identity. This perspective is culturally ridiculous as Indian languages from Hindi, to Bengali to Telugu, spanning from the East to the South via North India, have all been influenced by the Persian language.[120] Nehru's case is not exemplary. But it mattered, since Nehru rose as an important figure in anticolonial and Indian politics. The accusation stems from a mindset that regards the idea of identity and belonging as something that must be shorn off all influences from other identities in the world. It is a territorial idea of (religious) identity. If liberals and Marxists share the discomfort about people asserting their ascriptive identities, the religious right suffers the reverse problem: they are suspicious of those who belong to a culturally eclectic identity. Modernity has presented us with the dilemma of what is often referred to as 'identity-crisis', being simultaneously an individual identity and a culturally rooted one.

The second aspect to Nehru's sense of belonging, quite fundamental to his self-identity, is that it does not fulfil the criteria of Michael Sandel's 'unencumbered self':[121] the free, rationalist individual, a self that can dissociate itself from all constitutive (or inherited) ties of identity (or community), a self-producing being of rational choices, someone intellectually sovereign.

Nehru believed in a rationalist self (with an 'anchor of precise objective knowledge tested by reason'[122]). When it comes to his cultural identity, the question of belonging is inevitably paramount. Belonging is not a matter of choice. In Nehru's case it is partly *already chosen* by his ancestry. Nehru can't free himself, as he wrote, from 'past inheritance or my recent acquisitions'. Identity is a paradox and just like modernity, it is a matter of interpretation. They are both narratives of experience and imagination.

The paradox of identity is crucial to our understanding of the intellectual debates that have surrounded this particular aspect of political reality. Identity resists and challenges the totality of social realities and their corresponding concepts: the individual, class and national community. Identity cannot be subsumed by the idea of the 'people'. Identity is name, specificity, history and condition of marginalization. Identity breaks all ideas of oneness into two. This twoness *in itself* does not pose a threat to unity. The 'two-nation theory' that demanded Pakistan on the idea of a separate Muslim nation turns twoness into a rigid, non-negotiable political concept. The idea of unity, or oneness, in this case is premised upon religious identity. It rejects the possibility of twoness within. This is a perversion of the principle of twoness, which is the political and ethical basis of unity. Without two, there is no one. Otherness is the basis of unity and identity.

This understanding is lacking in Nehru due to his anxiety of national unity. It casts its shadow on his conception of secularism. Nehru extended the scope of secularism to include equality and justice. He has an open-arms idea of belonging, where the refugee, irrespective of identity, can be a part of the nation. The religious community is Nehru's black hole of reason.

In a circular on 5 August 1956, we read Nehru as he first creates the base for his argument of secularism: 'Politically, we are now a well-knit country . . . There are also many forces which help in this unifying process. But there are other forces also which tend to disintegrate and weaken this unity.'[123]

India is caught between two forces, according to Nehru, that are pulling it in two directions—towards unity and disunity. Against this backdrop, Nehru defines the meaning of secular in the Indian context with clarity:

> We call our state a secular one. The word 'secular' perhaps is not a very happy one. And yet, for want of a better, we have used it. What exactly does it mean? It does not obviously mean a state where religion as such is discouraged. It means freedom of religion and conscience, including freedom for those who may have no religion. It means free play for all religions, subject only to their not interfering with each other or with the basic conceptions of our state.[124]

Nehru is careful to make the important point that the word 'secular' in India should not give the wrong (or unhappy) impression that religion is discouraged, or that the State is against religion. That makes the Indian State much unlike a communist State, where the ideology of the State is opposed to the propagation—or even existence—of religion. Notice the emphasis on 'freedom' in the passage. Nehru equates Indian secularism with an active 'free play' of religion in the social and cultural sphere. However, the meaning of 'free play' and 'religion and conscience' must be taken more strictly, as Christophe Jaffrelot explained:

> The 1950 Constitution, strongly influenced by Nehru, did not recognise religious communities but only individuals, to whom it guaranteed in Article 25 'freedom of conscience and the right freely to profess, practice and propagate religion'. This ideal concept of religion as a private matter implied a reduction in its sphere of influence.[125]

From a rationalist perspective, the idea of conscience as a moral source can only be grounded in the individual. Communities can have sentiments, but not conscience.[126] Any interference of religion is strictly prohibited when it comes to the State. The boundary between what is religious and what is secular is clearly drawn at that point.

In Nehru's secular idea of the State, it is not religion but the community that is discouraged.

To draw a contrast, in a long statement made by Muhammad Iqbal in 1944 in a debate with Nehru on religion and orthodoxy, he wrote, 'In the history of Muslim political experience the separation has meant only a separation of functions, not of ideas.'[127] Iqbal is not hinting at the theological nexus between religion and the modern state as has been pointed by European thinkers. He is rather saying that the functions of the state are mediated by the religious sensibility of the people executing them. There is a degree of instrumentality at play. This creates a duality in the secular function of the state.

Nehru is interested in defining secularism in normative terms. He expands the meaning of the secular to include caste:

> The word 'secular' . . . conveys the idea of social and political
> equality. Thus, a caste-ridden society is not properly secular. I
> have no desire to interfere with any person's belief, but when
> those beliefs become petrified in caste divisions, undoubtedly
> they affect the social structure of the state. They prevent us
> from realizing the idea of equality which we claim to place
> before ourselves. They interfere in political matters, just as
> communalism interferes . . . [Communalism is] a negation of
> nationalism and of the national state.[128]

It is striking that Nehru expands the meaning of secularism to
include equality. Caste hierarchy is not secular. What Nehru seeks
to imply by connecting secularism and equality is that religious
freedom cannot exist in a deep sense, without its corresponding
value of equality. If hierarchies exist within a religious community,
it means it does not practice or live by the freedom it seeks in the
world. If people belonging to a religious community aren't treated
with equal respect and do not share the same sense of mutual
dignity, there is evidently no freedom within that community. If
a religious group wants equal treatment, it must treat members
within itself in the same manner. This is more than a normative
prescription. This is an ethical expectation, where (social)
difference based on hierarchy is sought to be abolished. The
modern democratic State is the highest organization of power,
law-making body and arbiter of values. Equality is one of its
enshrined principles.

Nehru goes ahead to equate inequality within a religious
community to his other central problem of political demands
made by a community. To pit communalism against nationalism
is a Nehruvian error in a country like India where minorities are
unequally poised vis-à-vis political power. To say that religion is
not discouraged is one thing, and to be unwilling to address the

political issues of a religious community is another. To remind the reader, the term 'communalism' has been understood and framed since the 1920s, as a problem associated primarily with minority politics.

Nehru's source of discomfort seems to be that if the State gets involved in favouring the cause of a religious minority *politically*, it will be a dangerous compromise and the blurring of its secularity. It may also end up unwittingly encouraging a majoritarian backlash. This is a legitimate liberal worry, except that it has remained incapable of addressing the real issue behind this problem. The real issue does not have to do with the political demands of the minority, but with the limits of the liberal secular State. The disengaged posture of neutrality espoused by the liberal State in matters pertaining to religion and community allows the problem of representation and rights to remain. It is an ostrich posture (of denial) that does the liberal State no good.

Akeel Bilgrami believes Nehru's neutrality-based statist approach 'is an imposition rather in the sense that it assumed that *secularism stood outside the substantive arena of political commitments*'.[129] He critiques Nehru, not for his secular approach, but 'with imposing a non-negotiated secularism'.[130]

Nehru believes in this policy because he is not just circumspect, but suspicious of religious groups making demands that are antithetical to the unity (and hence the political legitimacy) of the nation state. After a point that can never be cleanly marked—the politics of difference for Nehru merges into the politics of (a desire for) separation. This may well be a paranoia that comes from the failure to prevent Partition. The Muslim League had come to epitomize an illiberal position after it propounded the two-nation theory, based on religion. Nehru thought Jinnah's idea of the two-nation theory 'gave body to a metaphysical conception'.[131] Just before he made that remark, Nehru conceded that '[w]hat is a nation', and what explains or defines 'national consciousness' are questions involving 'theoretical abstractions'.[132]

The point is that nationalism and its so-called opposite communalism are both constructs born out of the modern political imagination where an anti-colonial movement took place in a multi-religious society. The anti-colonial movement in India was not one movement but a multiple one, with internal contestations between them.

'A Haunted Age': Behind the First Amendment

The First Amendment to India's new Constitution, moved by Nehru in 1951, challenged the force of constitutionality and Fundamental Rights. It has been a matter of serious debate for scholars and commentators. However, a key *political* aspect of the right to free speech and secularism pertinent to this debate has not been properly addressed.

The Constitution (First Amendment) Act, 1951, made new provisions for certain laws. The first was the granting of special rights and privileges to the Scheduled Castes and Tribes, by the introduction of a special clause (4) to Article 15 (that originally prohibited discrimination on the basis of race, caste, sex, religion, etc.), which created room for the State to make special provisions to 'socially and educationally backward classes of citizens'.[133] This was in accordance with India's commitment to affirmative action, or positive discrimination.[134] Those who faced the hurdle of power and hardship in the social order could bridge the gap of opportunities. It marked a—*necessary*—departure from the liberal principle of formal equality (derived from Aristotle) that treats the individual citizen as the sole, privileged subject in the modern nation state. Affirmative action is necessary to guarantee social equality. To grant individuals equal rights does not take away the importance, or necessity, of addressing social inequality.

The other provision was upholding of land reforms, or the right of the State to acquire individual property by the insertion of two provisions—Articles 31A and 31B—in the article relating to the right to property. Limits were posed to the idea of individual rights along with class privilege regarding holding of property. The clause of 'public purposes'[135] attached to the amendment, restricts State arbitrariness in the acquisition of property. The implementation of social reform is impossible without certain restrictions imposed on the right to property. Even if the right to property is upheld as a natural right in a bourgeois democracy, a political (and ethical) demand is made on the State to considerably limit feudal privileges (if not altogether abolish it). In a class society, the natural can't obfuscate the historical and the social. What falls under universally recognized rights must also take into account the universal history of exploitation.

Let me now turn to the amendment under concern: Giving freedom to the State—by replacing the existing clause (2) to Article 19—to execute an existing law or enact any new law for the purpose of imposing 'reasonable restrictions' on the right to freedom of expression 'in the interests of the security of the State, friendly relations with foreign States, public order, decency or morality, or in relation to contempt of court, defamation or incitement to an offence'.[136]

On 16 May 1951, Nehru tabled his fears regarding the future in a grave tone. He was worried about press reports that he felt were 'poisoning the mind of the younger generation, degrading their mental integrity and moral standards'.[137] He showed concern about 'the way untruth is bandied about and falsehood thrown about it'.[138] Nehru was referring specifically to two challenges, one from the left and another from the right. The left-wing challenge came from a communist ideologue, Romesh Thapar—printer, publisher and editor of the English weekly *Cross Roads*, printed in (then) Bombay. The journal is described as 'strongly anti-Congress'.[139] It spoke on the 'violation of civil liberties', 'police firings and jail deaths',[140] 'the US involvement in Korea and pro-Communist articles on Russia and China', and went as far as to offer strong 'criticism of the Draft Constitution, referred to often as the 'Slave Constitution'.[141] The Bombay Government's decision to ban *Cross Roads* was triggered by the reprint of a message by a trade union journal of China (*All-China Federation of Labour*), that condemned the 'reactionary' Indian government for cracking down on trade unionists and communists and called the act 'criminal'.[142] *Cross Roads* won the case in the Bombay High Court against the government's ban. In an editorial after the victory, Thapar wrote that the readers of the journal must 'decide the issue between People's Democracy and Congress fascism'.[143]

A free press in a democracy is expected to have a sense of commitment to the political system that makes its existence possible in the first place. If a journal finds the political regimes of communist countries, like the erstwhile Union of Soviet Socialist Republics (USSR) and China (where free press cannot exist), to be more worthy than a liberal democracy, there is a dubious lack of commitment to the very idea of the free press. *Cross Roads* won the case in court because of the freedom of speech guaranteed to Indian citizens.

To call the Indian Constitution a slave and the Congress fascist are ideologically motivated misrepresentations. It seeks to recreate a European model of communist politics after World War II, where the idea of a 'people's democracy' (a synonym for the socialist state, propagated by dictators like Stalin) was pitted against German fascism. Did the political reality in India warrant the need for such a model?

The right-wing challenge was partly triggered by the case of *Brij Bhushan* that involved the right-wing magazine, *Organiser*. The magazine faced a ban along with the Rashtriya Swayamsevak Sangha (RSS) in February 1948, after Gandhi's assassination, and reappeared in October.

Arudra Burra gives a detailed account of how the *Organiser* started off its second appearance on a mild tone, speaking about the 'denial of civil liberties' like its left counterpart and being critical of the Congress.[144] The tone shifted from December 1949, after Hindu-Muslim clashes took place in West Bengal where a Hindu political organization allegedly played a role.[145] It led to the migration of Muslims back to East Pakistan.

Nehru signed the Nehru–Liaquat Pact in April 1950, as a pledge to protect minorities in both countries. This led to the resignation of Syama Prasad Mookerjee from Nehru's Cabinet, as he doubted Pakistan's commitment.

Before it was signed, there was a pressure campaign in the media to dissuade Nehru from making the pact. In late February, the *Organiser* published a series of questions in the form of graphic descriptions and other details on Bengali Hindus facing violence in East Pakistan by an unnamed correspondent.[146] There was also a cartoon of Nehru as a cobra protecting Muslim evacuee property.[147]

The political narrative was back to the issues raised by some members during the Constituent Assembly Debates, on Muslim refugees and the question of citizenship and secularism.

The chief commissioner of Delhi imposed a restriction on the *Organiser*, under a section of the East Punjab Public Safety Act, 1949, where a provincial government was authorized for protecting 'public safety' and 'public order'.[148] K.R. Malkani, editor of the *Organiser*, took offence of the official notice against what he described as 'undisputed facts'.[149] One wonders why undisputed facts were printed in the form of questions rather than facts, that too by an anonymous correspondent.

When the case came up for hearing in the Supreme Court, the restriction on the magazine was declared unconstitutional and struck down—just like in the case of *Cross Roads*. It was a double victory for the cause of the free press.

It was in the backdrop of these events that Nehru, heading a provincial government, tabled the First Amendment to the Constitution in Parliament on 12 May 1951. The restriction on free speech that the First Amendment brought into the law raised a whole set of questions. Nivedita Menon in her 2004 essay finds the curbing of free speech as initiating a debate around two issues: one of them (that concerns us here) being 'the disjuncture between civil and political society'.[150] This distinction (and disjunction) between civil and political society can also be understood in terms of the double (or parallel) autonomy between the individual and the collective that Partha Chatterjee pointed out in the case of Ambedkar's argument for minority rights.

Ambedkar's intervention even here is important, as he supported the curbing of free speech in the First Amendment not to restore morality or strengthen State security but for the sake of 'public order' and 'incitement to offence' in cases 'where one community does something in order to harm or injure another community'.[151]

Even though Ambedkar had in mind the social boycott of Scheduled Castes by caste Hindus in the villages, his formulation of why the clause to restrict Article 19 (2) is necessary fits Nehru's specific concerns in this case.

After resigning from Nehru's cabinet in April 1950 in protest against Nehru's reconciliatory gestures with Pakistan, Syama Prasad Mookerjee began to sing the tunes of the Hindu Mahasabha—an organization he had resigned from earlier in

November 1948, after he felt there was no need for a separate body for Hindu interests.[152]

The Mahasabha had begun to speak of 'Akhand Bharat' (a pre-independent India) a few weeks before the pact was signed. Mookerjee added his voice to the propaganda, making speeches in (then) Calcutta on the plight of Hindu refugees in East Pakistan.[153] It led a disturbed Nehru to hold frantic correspondence with Patel. It was Patel who was the first to suggest the amendment. Writing to Nehru on 3 July 1950, Patel aired his helplessness about how to deal with a defiant press and Mookerjee. He ended the letter, saying: 'My own feeling is that very soon we shall have to sit down and consider constitutional amendments.'[154]

Between August 1950 and March 1951, Mookerjee made speeches both inside and outside Parliament 'bordering on calling for war between India and Pakistan and for their forcible reunification' as the only way to 'protect Pakistan's Hindu minority'.[155]

When the Bill for Amendment was tabled in Parliament, Mookerjee donned the garb of a passionate defender of free speech. Speaking on the initial motion, his rhetoric against Nehru appears like a shadow play between words and reality:

> I do not know why he has thrown up this challenge. Is it due to fear? Does he feel that he is incapable today to carry on the administration of the country unless he is clothed with more and more powers to be arbitrarily utilized so that his will may be the last word on the subject? Or is it his doubt in the wisdom of the people whose champion he has been all his life? Does he feel that the people of India have run amuck and cannot be trusted with the freedom that has been given to them?[156]

Mookerjee took recourse to sophistry to insinuate Nehru of authoritarian propensities. His rhetoric diverts the context of the amendment. The context was the call for war against Pakistan on the issue of minorities, and open threats to its sovereignty. The matter was not restricted to a problem of free speech, but of speech that undermines the principles of democracy. There is a strange contradiction in Nehru being adjudged authoritarian in this case. *An authoritarian leader spreads fear in others. Nehru is being accused by Mookerjee of being in fear of others.* That is quite the opposite of being authoritarian. Nehru's fear was the possibility of war. Is it wrong to discourage people from the mentality of war?

Nehru was not amending free speech to gain political control of his opponents. He was worried about the effects of war propaganda. When Mookerjee raises the question of Nehru's fear, what is he referring to? What does Nehru fear? It is, precisely, the fear of political leaders asking for war. Is that fear legitimate?

Mookerjee's use of 'people' is hyperbolic. It is not the people of India whose wisdom the prime minister doubted, but responsible political leaders waging war slogans. Nehru was tackling the Jekyll and Hydes of Indian politics.

Mookerjee decried the hasty tampering of a Fundamental Right like free speech, before it was put to the test of democracy. Taken by itself, the argument merits serious consideration. It is the politics behind that argument that muddies the waters.

Mookerjee went on to admit (and confront) the real reason behind what he knew prompted Nehru to the desperate option of Amending the new Constitution:

> I do not know whether it relates to the demand which is made in certain quarters about a possible reunion of India and Pakistan. I know the Prime Minister holds very strong views about it . . . But if I hold the contrary view . . . that *this partition has been a mistake and has to be annulled some day* or other why

should I not have a right to say that? . . . Why should I not have the right to agitate for it?[157]

This open admission warrants more attention (and discussion) than the rhetoric on free speech. It is not just 'contrarian view' to not accept a neighbourly nation's sovereignty and acknowledge the limit to one's own. Partition was a historical fact that Mookerjee thought could be annulled only by war. He did not think on the more important issue: Will war annul what caused Partition? War is not the annulment of political animosity. War is a return to the origin of conflict.

In a letter dated 16 February 1950, writing to the chief ministers on why the proponents of Akhand Bharat are entertaining a bad idea, Nehru wrote:

> Their talk of putting an end to partition is foolish to the extreme . . . If by any chance partition was ended, while present passions last on either side, it would mean tremendous new problems for us to face. We would be worse off than ever.[158]

Mookerjee's nationalism was focused on territoriality. Territory poses a limited situation and determines the reason behind the nation's paranoia. The paranoia of nations is territorial. To make war a political demand is neither liberal nor democratic. That too when a nation has just come into being by paying a very heavy cost, with millions of lives lost or impaired. Nehru's nervous determination to curb such war-speech in the public domain is understandable. Defending the Amendment Bill, Nehru said in Parliament:

> We live in a haunted age. I do not know how many hon. Members have that sense and that feeling—we in this country or in the world—of ghosts and apparitions surrounding us,

ideas, passions, hatred, violence, preparations for war, many things which you cannot grip, nevertheless which are more dangerous than other things.[159]

This is not hyperbole. Nehru is addressing the political atmosphere where ideologies of war are refusing to give a thought to democracy and are trying to destabilize it at its moment of inception. What is the age haunted by? It is haunted by 'ghosts' (of partition, war) that political reason cannot exorcize. Rather, these ghosts enter and manipulate the domain of political reason.

Nehru's fears regarding the dark political shadow looming over the times drew a sharp response from Mookerjee. 'You cannot pass or amend a Constitution to fight with "ghosts," he warned Nehru, likening him to the Prince of Denmark fighting imaginary troubles in Shakespeare's *Hamlet*.'[160]

Nehru wasn't delusional. His ghosts were not imaginary. In a letter to Patel, on 3 July 1950, Nehru wrote: 'I find no legal powers to deal with either Press or men like Syama Prasad Mookerjee.'[161]

Nehru's fears of Mookerjee were exaggerated. But the basis of the fear was not. Nehru was not trying to secure civil society by putting curbs on political society, but rather make politics across ideologies more sensitive to democracy. The newly paved ground of Indian democracy was still in a fragile state.

Nehru's reasons of limiting free speech do not come from liberal-statist concerns. He is worried about the possibility of war, the breakdown of community ties, and the fate of minorities in both Pakistan and India. In other words, Nehru's worry is political and ethical. Nehru, the sober rationalist, was rattled by the rawness of the political challenge posed by anti-minoritarian ideologues. Mookerjee could sense that weakness. Nehru took a legal route to take care of a political problem. The law of politics can't always be managed by the politics of law. It was an injudicious method to solve a political problem. It lacked prudence. The case, however, made Nehru overcome the 'Hamlet-like hesitations'[162] that Walter Crocker observed in him.

The idea of free speech is often defended in a sacrosanct and matter-of-fact manner, without unpacking its meaning and what limits it.

Article 19 of the Universal Declaration of Human Rights (UDHR) speaks of the freedom of speech and expression. By language and conception, the right to free speech in the UDHR is granted to the individual. This right is ideally considered unconstrained. Salman Rushdie put it with memorable bluntness in his essay, 'In Good Faith': 'What is freedom of expression? Without the freedom to offend it ceases to exist. Without the freedom to challenge, even to satirize all orthodoxies, including religious orthodoxies, it ceases to exist.'[163]

Rushdie defines freedom of expression, as a freedom of language to dismantle the discourse (and establishments) of power. He is arguing in favour of a modern force of heterodoxical (or heretical) imagination against old orthodoxies. This idea is not entirely Western or even rationalist. It can take the form of alternate, critical discourses within tradition. Rushdie tries to define the larger context in similar terms:

> The Satanic Verses is, in part, a secular man's reckoning with the religious spirit. It is by no means always hostile to faith . . . Yet the novel does contain doubts, uncertainties, even shocks that may well not be to the liking of the devout. Such methods have, however, long been a legitimate part of even Islamic literature.[164]

Rushdie is defining 'secular' here as non-believer, and holds the view that a secular, non-believing individual has the right to challenge a community of faith. This idea goes beyond the idea of orthodox power as it involves the (imagined or real) community *as a whole*. The individual here is understood as a rights-bearing subject who must possess unconstrained freedom to imagine and express her mind about anything, including a belief shared by millions of people.

I have posed the issue of free speech using Rushdie, not to offer my conclusions on this individual-versus-community debate on freedom of expression. Rushdie's example can be contrasted with Nehru's context during the making of the First Amendment. The problem Nehru faced—and what concerns us at the moment—was what we understand today as 'hate speech'.

The amendment on free speech in 1951 was not wisely worded. To curb speech 'in the interests of the security of the State' further strengthens the controversial 1860 colonial law of sedition (Section 124A of the Indian Penal Code). Since 2014, the law of sedition has been manipulated and used as a tool of legal coercion against citizens (activists, writers, artists, journalists, and even politicians) who spoke against majoritarian violence and intimidation in our polity, as well as in public culture and institutions. In contrast, free flowing hate speech by right-wing ideologues against minorities and anti-majoritarian voices have been allowed to thrive.

In May 2019, the United Nations Secretary-General, António Guterres, published a statement on hate speech—calling it 'a menace to democratic values, social stability and peace'.[165] He mentioned social media and other platforms being used to promote 'bigotry' and wrote: 'Public discourse is being weaponized for political gain with incendiary rhetoric that stigmatizes and dehumanizes minorities, migrants, refugees, women and any so-called "other".'[166]

The Secretary-General's concern has been part of high reality in India since 2016. What is interesting here is to note how Rushdie's 'freedom to offend' takes on a different meaning when the idea is pitted against minoritarian identities by a free and mobile army of right-wing ideologues. Once the register of free speech shifts from the individual to the community, other considerations come into the picture. The matter gets complicated, as much as disturbing. When xenophobia translates into violence, it does not just challenge mindsets but endangers lives.

We confront here the other pole of free speech, where hate speech poses its limits. Nehru was confronting a similar situation of hate speech in 1950–51 without the necessary vocabulary available to him. No Constitutional guarantee or law can stop an elected government in a representative democracy to power its way against dissidents.

What can be affirmed in hindsight is that Nehru's tampering with a Constitutional right sought to make space for restrictions to free speech so that minorities in India feel secure. Lacking a clear objective, Nehru was desperately willing to curb civil liberties to secure social and political peace.

3

Culture and the 'Urge towards Synthesis'

Early in *The Discovery*, Nehru took the example of the 'Pathan of the North-West and the Tamil in the far South'[1] to illustrate how India's diversity conceals a deeper reality. No two people could be outwardly more dissimilar—'in face and figure, food and clothing, and, of course, language'—and *yet* 'no mistaking the impress of India on the Pathan, as this is obvious on the Tamil'.[2]

Before Islam appeared, the mixed races in Afghanistan were influenced by Buddhist and Hindu cultures, and these, according to Nehru, formed part of the 'mental background'[3] of the people. Nehru is not so much essentializing the meaning of something amorphously understood as Indian culture. He seems to be suggesting something more interesting; not just about his idea of culture but also his idea of what is Indian.

Nehru seems to understand culture as a matter of a certain experience, something that involves an *encounter*. In this case, the encounter between the Pathans and the Hindu and Buddhist cultures produced what can be called Indian culture. For Nehru, it was a historically formative experience that defined the characteristics and attitude of a people that later embraced Islam. To claim that the Muslim Pathans who came later into the story did not lose the earlier cultural ties they shared with the Tamils is to see cultural life as distinct from religious belief. This also meant that the Muslim Pathans were unlike the Muslims of other places.

At the anti-CAA protest site at Delhi's Shaheen Bagh in February 2020, the classical singer and activist, T.M. Krishna, sang the famous ghazal 'Hum Dekhenge' (We shall see . . .)—by the renowned Urdu poet from Pakistan Faiz Ahmed Faiz—in his native Tamil, and two other languages from south India, Kannada and Malayalam, besides the original Urdu.[4] Faiz was not Pathan, and Urdu is not Pashtun, but matters are close. There is a cultural history that enables the event in this case, given a certain leftwing revolutionary trope of the poem, and Krishna's own political sensibility. The singing artist is following a tradition of translatability. It prompts associations across different languages and cultural locations. India is a nation in translation.

Like Nehru said in *The Discovery*:

I think that at almost any time in recorded history an Indian would have felt more or less at home in any part of India, and would have felt as a stranger and alien in any other country . . . Those who professed a religion of non-Indian origin or, coming to India, settled down there, became distinctively Indian in the course of a few generations, such as Christians, Jews, Parsees, Moslems. Indian converts to some of these religions never ceased to be Indians on account of a change of their faith. They were looked upon in other countries as Indians and foreigners, even though there might have been a community of faith between them.[5]

There was something of a loosely defined characteristic that characterized who an Indian is, which left a recognizable imprint on the inhabitants of India. What is Indian was not defined by religion—as converts to other religions and settlers who belonged to other regions (and religions) came to share similar cultural traits in India—and could be demarcated from the rest of the world. The meaning of being Indian was both elusive and concrete, and yet could not be restricted to faith or any particular marker of identity.

Nehru further drove the point home: 'An Indian Christian is looked upon as an Indian wherever he may go. An Indian Moslem is considered an Indian in Turkey or Arabia or Iran, or any other country where Islam is the dominant religion.'[6]

Nehru is provoking us with the observation that India, or Indian, is a valid anthropological construct. Cultures are a combination of the material and the mental. This idea of culture is different from the relation between the material and the mental in structuralist discourse, where social relations (based on relations of production) are involved. This also does not go by the Marxist hierarchy between material (as base) and mental or cultural (as superstructure).

Nehru, the Weberian

Nehru's understanding of culture, I would argue, is Weberian. The Weber I would invoke here is not the Weber who wrote on India, but on his broader perspective on culture. There are different aspects to Weber's understanding of culture. I would like to focus on two of them.

One, that culture retains a specificity that has a bearing on historical changes. Friedrich Jäger has written about the many functional aspects that culture fulfils in Weber's thought:

motivational or utopian functions, disciplinary functions, stabilizing and stratifying functions, legitimising and integrating functions[7]. More fundamentally, culture has a 'meaning-generating' function, against the 'meaninglessness'[8] of history, individual life, and death. Renarde Freire Nobre draws our attention to how Weber was vehemently against the 'universal and totalizing visions' embedded in the 'monocausal and "prophetic" nature of historical materialism'.[9] For Weber, the 'meaningful individualities' of cultures are more significant than the 'general laws' of history.[10] This brings Weber closer to Nietzsche, who also did not cater to the Hegelian idea of world history. Weber's understanding complicates the Marxist notion where history is *solely* produced by the contradiction of social forces. In his study, the Protestant ethic and 'rational organization'[11] of life and labour facilitated the birth of capitalism in the West.[12] The Weberian perspective is that culture *produces* history as much as socio-economic factors. In *The Discovery*, Nehru treats culture as a determining feature of Indian history.

The second idea of Weber that resonates in Nehru is reason, or rationality being the 'universal organizative principle'[13] in the movement of modern cultures. This assumption gives the idea of culture its paradoxical quality, where specificity is understood through the principle of reason, a larger force or tendency at work in the modern world. Rationality works as a value when it comes to culture, apart from the value that constitutes the meaning of culture in its specificity. We are dealing with a framework of double value regarding culture. For Weber, rationality adds value to culture as a means to knowledge and provides meanings, or tools, of evaluation. Reason is an *exterior value* that Weber attaches with cultures. Like many Western modernists of his time, the German thinker is keen to situate—and consequently, establish—the value of reason as a normative for cultures to assist a comparative understanding. By doing this, however, Weber inadvertently creates a series of conceptual dichotomies: rational/irrational, specific/universal, and exterior/interior. These create specific problems in our understanding of culture.

Nehru is also prone to these Weberian dichotomies, which are a product of Enlightenment rationality. We shall see how Nehru navigates his thoughts through the rationalist biases that he inherits from Western modernity, and whether he is able to overcome them at certain moments.

In his bid to define (the impact of) culture, Nehru places the 'mental' over the material immediacy of a social structure. The overall formulation is not Marxist, in the sense that the meaning of culture, for Nehru, is not to be derived from—isn't reflected upon or to be understood through—the materialist prism of social hierarchies (or relations) and productivity.

Nehru situates culture outside the mediational or deterministic logic of the base/superstructure model. There is a sense of simultaneity and reciprocity between culture and social reality. One may well influence the other. Nehru seems to understand the historical journey of culture in India (or India's cultural history), as following a certain principle or tendency of seeking and assimilation.

Culture as *Encounter*

India, for Nehru, is where a special kind of *encounter* takes place among cultures. These encounters determine Indian history.

There is an interesting speculative aspect in Nehru's idea of culture. It grants a unique trait to Nehru's anthropological insight. Remember the question Nehru asks himself in the early pages of *The Discovery*:

Did I know India?—I who presumed to scrap much of her past heritage? There was a great deal that had to be scrapped, that must be scrapped; but surely India could not have been what she undoubtedly was, and could not have continued a cultured existence for thousands of years, if she had not possessed something very vital and enduring, something that was worthwhile. What was this something?[14]

Nehru begins with a sense of humility but a humility that is paradoxically arrogant, as he confesses to his desire to 'scrap' portions of India's 'heritage' from the national syllabus. But despite his modernist arrogance (shared by almost all liberals and Marxist thinkers in India), the good thing about Nehru is that he persists with his curiosity and wonder regarding the longevity of India's cultural vitality. He wanted to know the secret of the 'something' about *how* India's pre-modern culture endured across history, and *what was it* that was responsible for this endurance:

India was changing and progressing all the time. She was coming into intimate contact with the Persians, the Egyptians, the Greeks, the Chinese, the Arabs, the Central Asians, and the peoples of the Mediterranean. But though she influenced them and was influenced by them, her cultural basis was strong enough to endure. What was the secret of this strength? Where did it come from?[15]

Nehru offers the answer to the question. The capacity to absorb cultural influences and create a new confluence is the open secret of Indian history. The Indo-Aryans, who themselves came to India from elsewhere, encountered people from various parts of the world who came for travel and trade. These encounters produced new influences that did not displace the existing culture in India, but rather added to it. This is what made Nehru write these famous poetic lines on India:

> She was like some ancient palimpsest on which layer upon layer of thought and reverie had been inscribed, and yet no succeeding layer had completely hidden or erased what had been written previously. All of these existed in our conscious or subconscious selves, though we may not have been aware of them, and they had gone to build up the complex and mysterious personality of India.[16]

In Nehru's imagination, India's 'mysterious personality' was a thing of wonder and curiosity. The cultural script of India's history, both vanishing and inerasable, is full of impressions and erasures, signs and traces that succeed each other in time. It is reminiscent of Homi K. Bhabha's critical observation regarding the 'impossibly romantic and excessively metaphorical' image of the nation, where 'nations, like narratives lose their origins in the myths of time and only fully realize their horizons in the mind's eye'.[17] Nehru's imagery is, however, not fixed in any indigenous theory of origins but suggestive of the cultural encounters that provided "the layer upon layer of thought" across historical time.

Nehru's mentalist image of the nation in its language and cognitive claims, breaks out of the limitations imposed by rationalist reconstruction. In the world of capitalist (or even socialist) modernity, nations are the grandest myth made real. They resist being reduced to a pragmatic construct based on the double logic that people need a territory based on ethnicity, and a market based on the connective threads of modern economy. Beyond ethnic ties and a purely market logic, nations are the 'imagined communities' that Benedict Anderson theorized.[18]

Nehru's interesting ambivalence is that he is keen to pursue the secret vitality that made Indian culture outlive the dust and death of centuries, and yet he felt that much of what Indian culture retains through historical metamorphosis must be let go of. Nehru wanted to retain the vitality alone and not what it produced. In other words, it was necessary to imbibe the inherent *capacity* of Indian culture to adapt, but not necessarily the *content* of that adaptation. The capacity was the historical life force of Indian culture, but the content was dated and must be judged by the demands of time. Nehru is quite firm about this distinction, as he intensifies it:

> (The) essential ideals of Indian culture are broad-based and can be adapted to almost any environment. The bitter conflict between science and religion which shook up Europe in the nineteenth century would have no reality in India, nor would change based on the applications of science bring any conflict with those ideals . . . It is probable that in this process many vital changes may be introduced in the old outlook, but they will not be super-imposed from outside and will seem to *grow naturally* from the *cultural background* of the people.[19]

Nehru is optimistic that India's cultural vitality, the 'secret' capacity to absorb new thought will 'naturally' graduate into modernity. India was better poised than nineteenth-century Europe to welcome science and rationality. Nehru considered this cultural background as a trans-historical phenomenon:

> I think that a country with a long cultural background and a common outlook on life develops a spirit that is peculiar to it and that is impressed on all its children, however much they may differ among themselves. Can anyone fail to see this

in China, whether he meets an old-fashioned mandarin or a Communist who has apparently broken with the past? It was this spirit of India that I was after.[20]

There is something culturally common between the mandarin and the communist in China. There is a layered secret of cultural habit and historical memory that the mandarin and the communist share between each other that they may not be aware of, and yet, it may be visible to the outsider. Cultural similarities, often invisible among those who share them, may be visible to others who are not part of that culture. The very recognition of similarity by the outsider shows how culture demarcates a distinction between those who share it and those who don't.

Nehru is also making a political comment. He believes communists in China haven't really broken their ties with the country's cultural history. Old habits do not disappear from indoctrination programmes like the miserable one that Mao se-Tung unleashed in the name of Cultural Revolution.[21]

Culture, as Nehru seems to understand, is not ideology or belief (modern or pre-modern, rational or religious). Culture is understood as an intense space or field of thought and art that is produced by people of a community. The impulse and form that shapes these cultural productions are diverse in nature. *Cultures are diverse from within.* In other words, cultures are *internally* diverse. Each culture is a field of diverse expressions by people belonging to a community. It is, therefore, natural to expect and desire that a certain harmony of diversity exists between cultures, as all cultures are both intrinsically and functionally diverse. Culture, unlike religion and ideology, is not about *just one thing.*

To encounter a culture is to encounter diversity. That is why the historical encounter between cultures holds the promise of mutually engaging varieties of artistic and intellectual production.

The hybrid nature of culture is argued from this fact: cultures are hybrids.

This anthropological perspective challenges the claims of autochthony or indigeneity, made by cultural purists, often to serve the politics of ethnicity. To deny the contribution of migrants to the script and movement of cultures is a denial of the natural principle of history. The encounter between cultures is a historical fact.

In ethical philosophy, the idea of the encounter is traced to Martin Buber's statement in his classic work, *I and Thou*: 'All actual life is encounter.'[22] Without getting into the metaphysics of the (interiorized) self and other relationship, it is possible to draw an exterior—'actual'—connection between Buber's matter of fact yet ethical reminder of our dialogic history, or a history of encounters. Emanuel Levinas derives from Buber: 'Man does not meet, he is the meeting.'[23] Meeting is better translated as 'encounter'.[24] What we may derive from Levinas via Buber is that *cultures are encounters* (in themselves). Deriving from Buber, Levinas finds the nature of such an encounter enabled by a 'double movement' of proximity and distance, where 'philosophy is identifiable with anthropology'.[25] Cultures are relational entities where the idea of individuality, or uniqueness, is not derived from a relation to itself, but in relation to other cultures.

This idea finds resonance in Ranjit Hoskote and Ilija Trojanow. They affirm the impact of cultural encounters through 'confluence', a fact that is often 'concealed' to foster 'homogenous foundational myths'.[26] The authors reiterate that cultural confluences have occurred in history through conflict and hence not to be understood as a utopia 'brought together into a single polity'.[27] The mode of confluence is determined by the 'mobility of people, ideas, goods and services', and follows the logic of 'mercantile complicity'.[28] The fundamental impulse remains that of 'basic curiosity and intellectual generosity'.[29] The modern West imbibes the sense of curiosity that profited pre-modern cultures, but it lacks their generosity.

Nehru's approach to India's cultural past(s) is diachronous. He is interested in deciphering the continuities of culture through its historical journey and survival across time. American cultural anthropologist Alfred L. Kroeber calls the diachronous approach 'comparative or dynamically historical'.[30] Koreber divides the diachronous view into monistic and pluralistic approaches. The monistic approach, with Voltaire as its exemplar, tends to separate historical stages while adhering to the idea of progress.[31] In the pluralistic approach, heralded by Herder, the 'philosophic . . . recedes . . . before the empirical'.[32] Nehru, as we shall see in some detail in the next chapter on history, does not adhere to both approaches. He has a strong notion of progress when it comes to comparing modern civilization with the past and its values. But he also considers the lack of modernity in relation to a valuable cultural phenomenon in the past:

> There is something lacking in all this progress, which can neither produce harmony between nations nor within the spirit of man. Perhaps more *synthesis* and a little humility towards the wisdom of the past, which, after all, is the accumulated experience of the human race, would help us to gain a new perspective and greater harmony. That is especially needed by those peoples who live a fevered life in the present only and have almost forgotten the past.[33]

Nehru's view draws close to what Charles Taylor describes as the Romantic subjectivist stance or what he calls 'the inward turn'.[34] The realization is that modernity can overcome its lack by drawing meaningful resources from the past:

> The present age is indeed spiritually indignant. We in our time
> need to recover the past in order to attain fullness. But this
> is not so much because history has meant decline, as because
> the *fullness of meaning* isn't available with the resources of a
> single age. And what is more . . . we can *recapture the past*,
> or rather, make the great moments and achievements of other
> times come alive in ours.[35]

Nehru has a similar sense of 'fullness' in mind as he writes here
in *The Discovery*: '[The] infinite, eternal and unchanging truth
cannot be apprehended in its fullness by the finite mind of man
which can only grasp, at most, some small aspect of it limited by
time and space, and by the state of development of that mind and
the prevailing ideology of the period.'[36] Nehru echoes Taylor's
Romantic subjectivist figure when he acknowledges that the
experience of fullness is 'limited by time and space', and warrants
our opening the doors to the past when necessary. If progress was
missing in the history of pre-modern times, the sense of harmony
and the spirit of cultural synthesis were missing in modernity.
Nehru's idea was, in this sense, more balanced than the monistic
approach. And his narrative of history was equally balanced
between the philosophic and the empirical. Between the details of
historical events, Nehru was always keen to pause over intellectual,
social and cultural values that he felt were worthy enough to retain
in modernity.

Sources of Indian Culture

It will be instructive to dwell a bit on the specificities of other
cultures that people in India encountered and made their own.
Before we encounter Nehru's description of the story of influence,
here is a description of the geo-cultural crust or source of history:

> The story of the Ganges, from her source to the sea, from old times to new, is the story of India's civilization and culture, of the rise and fall of empires, of great and proud cities, of the adventure of man and the quest of the mind which has so occupied India's thinkers, of the richness and fulfilment of life as well as its denial and renunciation, of ups and downs, of growth and decay, of life and death.[37]

The river is a rich and evocative metaphor of history, of geo-cultural time, a natural witness to the fate of human lives. It also marks (sacred) territory.

Mirza Ghalib's poem on Banaras, 'Chirag-e-Dair'/'Temple Lamps' recollects his four-month sojourn in the city in the late half of 1827. In his memorable ode to the old city that he calls 'the Kaaba of Hind',[38] Ghalib imbues it with the meanings of sacred geography. The carefree presence of courtesans dazzles Ghalib and he paints them as part of the spiritual charm of Banaras. The 'Ganga-mirror'[39] reflects the city's beauty. Banaras and Ganga are a double-image of a sacred paradise locked in time. In the spirit of ethnography, Ghalib asked a learned seer why unlike other places in the world, Banaras was not yet besieged by political and moral decadence (in the form of patricide, fratricide and loss of political unity), and the seer told him it was because God was fond of this place.[40] He found the spectacle of life in Banaras more inspiring than the decaying citadel of Bahadur Shah Zafar's Delhi. Ghalib was so inspired that he 'almost wished that he could have left his own religion to pass his life on the bank of the Ganga with prayer beads, a sacred thread, and a mark on his forehead'.[41] For a courtly poet of the Mughal Empire, Ghalib's desire to contemplate as a sadhu beside the Ganga is an exemplary moment in India's cultural history. It attests the Nehruvian idea of *historical encounter* in India, where people were cultural converts. In Banaras, Ghalib experienced a vibrant tranquility that was missing in Delhi. Cultural conversions are a matter of place as much as belief. Ghalib was a pilgrim who had fortuitously found the place that tempted him to become a sadhu. It was made possible by a deep sense of proximity and love. Cultures are invitations.

Now let us turn to some concrete examples that Nehru refers to in *The Discovery*, regarding cultural interactions between India and other civilizations.

Nehru notes that Panini, the Sanskrit grammarian who lived between the fourth and sixth centuries BCE, mentions the Greek script in his treatise, which suggests the possibility of contacts with the Greeks even before Alexander's entry.[42] Both Chandragupta Maurya and his teacher in statecraft and war, Chanakya, met the Greeks in Taxila.[43] The Greek traveller-historian Megasthenes, who was sent to India as an ambassador by Seleucus, wrote that the wine served to Chandragupta Maurya and the women who served him the wine, both came from Greece.[44]

Nehru mentions the Iranian scholar-traveller Al-Biruni, who in his visit to India in the eleventh century, discovered 'common features' between the Greek philosophy he studied in Baghdad and Indian philosophy, including 'Sanskrit books that deal with Greek and Roman astronomy'.[45] In Al-Biruni's *India*, he mentions that the idea of the '*First Cause*' of material reality was similar in Hindus, Greeks and the Sufis.[46] Al-Biruni draws another parallel that Hindus, Greeks and 'heathen Arabs' considered idols as 'mediators between themselves and the *First Cause*'.[47]

After the fall of the Maurya Empire and the advent of the Sunga dynasty, the Greek army led by Menander attacked Pataliputra but was defeated and the Greek king turned Buddhist. 'From the fusion of Indian and Greek cultures rose', writes Nehru, 'the Graeco-Buddhist art of Gandhara, the region covering

Afghanistan and the frontier.'[48] This example is also acknowledged by Kroeber, who writes in the context of cultural encounters:

> One style can influence another, and such phenomena of contact and derivation are of course noted, and traced by anthropologists and historians of art; for instance the impingement of Greek on northwest Indian Gandhara sculpture in the early Christian centuries.[49]

Nehru mentions the 'granite pillar called the Heliodorus column, dating from the first century B.C., at Besnagar, near Sanchi in Central India, bearing an inscription in Sanskrit'.[50]

This told Nehru of the 'absorption of Indian culture'[51] by the Greeks. To mark a point of difference with both Greece and Iran, Nehru observed that enough references in both Greek and Persian literature show there was 'romantic approval' of homosexual relations.[52] There was no such sign of acceptance of same-sex relations and culture in Sanskrit literature during this period, according to Nehru.[53] He makes a rather awkward comparison vis-à-vis slave labour in Greece with India's caste system, calling the latter 'infinitely better.'[54] Despite the occupational fixity, Nehru thought the casts system still 'led to a high degree of specialization and skill in handicrafts and craftsmanship'.[55] Such comparisons of hierarchies that are structures of humiliation cannot be measured in terms of the difference in the respective skills of those who bear the brunt of that hierarchy, and the nature and quality of their production. Elsewhere in *The Discovery*, Nehru acknowledged that the logic of separation in caste introduced 'a separation of theoretical and scholastic learning from craftsmanship'.[56] This is the enforced division of labour that, in Ambedkar's incisive words, is 'also a division of labourers'.[57] The problem with Nehru's comparative logic is that it is a lack of ethical sensibility to make objectivist arguments regarding subjective experiences of graded inequality. One experience cannot be better or worse than another.

It appears from Nehru's account that the mark of Greek culture in India was largely restricted to sensuous pleasure and the influence of Buddhism on Greek rulers. Except a crucial and unexpected addition to Hindu culture via Buddhism that was facilitated by Greece, Nehru tells us, 'Greek artistic influence in Afghanistan and round about the frontier' was the source of 'Apollo-like statues of the Bodhisattvas' and finally statues of the Buddha himself.[58] We learn that the 'word for an image or statue in Persian and in Hindustani still is But (like put) derived from Buddha'.[59]

According to Nehru, the Indo-Aryans had 'elaborated' in the Vedas the ideas of the Avesta.[60] He wrote:

> The Vedic religion had much in common with Zoroastrianism, and Vedic Sanskrit and the old Pahlavi, the language of the Avesta, closely resemble each other. Classical Sanskrit and Persian developed separately but many of their root-words were common.[61]

Nehru finds the Iranian influence 'continuous' in successive periods as under the Afghan and Mughal regimes, 'Persian was the court language.'[62]

India clearly had ancient ties with Iran's pre-Islamic culture, with both Zoroastrians and the Indo-Aryans being fire-worshippers, hence had certain common conceptions of worship. The ties with the Old Persian language that changed forms continued with the coming of the Muslims. We have many words from Persian in the Indian vernaculars, and they date back to both the pre-Islamic and the Islamic era.

Nehru writes that the first contacts between the Chinese and Indians took place during the Kushan Empire. Taxila University was the meeting place where 'vigorous school of sculpture and painting arose as a result of their interactions'.[63] In recorded history, Kashyapa Matanga was the first Indian scholar to visit China in 67 AD, during the reign of Chinese emperor Ming Ti. After his visit, an estimated 30,000 Buddhist monks from India were found in the Lo Yang province. These monks carried manuscripts in the Sanskrit language, which they translated into Chinese and also wrote originally in Chinese. The 'two-way traffic'[64] between India and China led the famous travellers—Fa Hien in the fifth century and later, Hiuen Tsang in the seventh century—to travel across India and leave behind fascinating accounts of the time. Tsang travelled to central Asia and reached Iraq, chronicling the spread of Buddhism just before Islam would emerge in Arabia.[65] Nehru recounts an interesting anecdote:

Hsuan-Tsang himself remained in touch with India, exchanging letters with friends there and receiving manuscripts. Two interesting letters, originally written in Sanskrit, have been preserved in China. One of these was written in 654 A.C. [sic] by an Indian Buddhist scholar, Sthavira Prajnadeva, to Hsuan-Tsang. After greeting and news about common friends and their literary work, he proceeds to say: 'We are sending you a pair of white cloths to show that we are not forgetful. The road is long, so do not mind the smallness of the present. We wish you may accept it. As regards the Sutras and Shastras which you may require please send us a list. We will copy them and send them to you.' Hsuan-Tsang in his reply says: 'I learnt from an ambassador who recently came back from India that the great teacher Shilabhadra was no more. This news overwhelmed me with grief that knew no bounds . . . Among the Sutras and Shastras that I, Hsuan-Tsang, had brought with me I have already translated the Yogacharyabhumi-Shastra and other works, in all thirty volumes. I should humbly let you know that while crossing the Indus I had lost a load of sacred texts. I now send you a list of the texts annexed to this letter. I request you to send them to me if you get the chance. I am sending some small articles as presents. Please accept them.'[66]

This collegial affiliation between Chinese and Buddhist religious scholars sounds profoundly sincere and speaks well of the scholastic culture of those times. The acknowledgement of grief betrays deep affection. There is also an amiable sense of mutual respect in the relationship between Indian and Chinese scholars. There is a visible, scholastic commitment towards sacred and literary texts belonging to diverse traditions. It is a commitment to what in simple terms can be called a search for the meaning of human life. To look for that meaning across cultures in premodern times seems quite unarrogant and civilized compared to what the colonial West imposed over its subject peoples, as a superior system of knowledge.

Next is Nehru's account of India's defining historical encounter with Muslims: he understands from accounts of the Chinese traveller I-Tsing, who travelled to India around 671 BCE after Tsang's death, that there was 'regular navigation between Persia (Iran), India, Malaya, Sumatra, and China'.[67] The coming of Muslim rulers kept the Indo-Chinese conversation alive.

Nehru's account further reads:

Mohammed bin Tughlak, Sultan of Delhi (1326–51) sent the famous Arab traveller, Ibn Batuta, as ambassador to the Chinese court. Bengal had at that time shaken off the suzerainty of Delhi and became an independent sultanate. In the middle of the fourteenth century the Chinese court sent two ambassadors, Hu-Shien and Fin-Shien, to the Bengal Sultan.[68]

It is striking that after the persecution of Buddhist centres of learning between the tenth and twelfth centuries by Turkic-Afghan rulers, Tughlak initiated contact with the Buddhists. About the growth of Indo-Islamic culture in the north, Nehru mentions Akbar's reign as facilitating cross-cultural influences within a collaborative political design:

> Akbar was an admirer of and felt a kinship with the Rajputs, and by his matrimonial and other policy he formed an alliance with the Rajput ruling classes which strengthened his empire greatly. This Mughal-Rajput co-operation, which continued in subsequent reigns, affected not only government and the administration and army, but also art, culture, and ways of living. The Mughal nobility became progressively Indianized and the Rajputs and others were influenced by Persian culture.[69]

Once again, language was at the centre of these mutual cultural influences:

> During the Mughal period large numbers of Hindus wrote books in Persian which was the official court language. Some of these books have become classics of their kind. At the same time Moslem scholars translated Sanskrit books into Persian and wrote in Hindi. Two of the best-known Hindi poets are Malik Mohammad Jaisi who wrote the 'Padmavat' and Abdul Rahim Khankhana, one of the premier nobles of Akbar's court and son of his guardian.[70]

One of the most shining examples of this mutual influence is Dara Shikoh's translation of 52 verses from the Upanishads into Persian, called *Sirr-I Akbar*, or 'The Great Secret'. The 'secret' refers to, in Jonardon Ganeri's scholarly study, a 'common subject matter'[71] between the holy Quran and the Upanishads. This suggests, according to Ganeri, a 'religious cosmopolitanism, a belief that there is a common spiritual heritage to all humanity'[72] and yet there is an important mark of difference: Ganeri agrees with Seyyed Nasr that Shikoh's translation 'does not at all indicate a syncretism', this is not bringing 'religious traditions into dialogue or conversation' but as 'drawing together different strands of a common resource'.[73] One can define culture in this and similar contexts as a field where the possibility of active translations between traditions has taken place.

Partly due to conversion and partly from a history of contact, Nehru writes:

> Hindus and Moslems in India developed numerous common traits, habits, ways of living and artistic tastes, especially in northern India—in music, painting, architecture, food, clothes, and common traditions . . . [They] joined each other's festivals and celebrations, spoke the same language, lived in more or less the same way, and faced identical economic problems.[74]

Nehru also mentions the important social aspect of how the coming of the Muslims led to conversions based on the principle of equality in Islamic society:

> The idea of the brotherhood of Islam and of the theoretical equality of its adherents made a powerful appeal, especially to those in the Hindu fold who were denied any semblance of equal treatment. From this ideological impact grew up various

movements aiming at a religious synthesis. Many conversions also took place but the great majority of these were from underprivileged castes, especially in Bengal. Some individuals belonging to the higher castes also adopted the new faith, either because of a real change of belief, or, more often, for political and economic reasons. There were obvious advantages in accepting the religion of the ruling power.

Those belonging to the privileged castes adopted Islam to maintain their privileges, while those at the bottom of the hierarchy converted for the sake of dignity and equality. There is a stark contrast in the ethical impulse behind what the underprivileged castes did, especially in Bengal, and privileged-caste Hindus. The interesting historical aspect here is the pre-modern nature of this ethical impulse towards equality that Islam provides people who suffered the experience of hierarchical exploitation and humiliation.

In a letter to Mohammad Sarfaraz Husain in Nainital, Swami Vivekananda writes from Almora on 10 June 1898:

> practical Advaitism, which looks upon and behaves to all mankind as one's own soul, was never developed among the Hindus universally. On the other hand, my experience is that if ever any religion approached to this equality in an appreciable manner, it is Islam and Islam alone.[75]

This is a striking admission from the high priest of Hindu revivalism. It is also noteworthy that Vivekananda upholds the (modern) value of social equality that he found in Islam as a concrete form of—and compliment to—spiritual equality.

Elsewhere in *The Discovery*, Nehru mentioned the fact of Hindustani classical music finding place in the Mughal court, its practitioners. Nehru mentions, 'Ibrahim Adil Shah, the ruler of Bijapur, [who] wrote a treatise in Hindi on Indian music',[76] and 'Amir Khusrau, a Turk . . . who lived in the fourteenth century during the reigns of several Afghan Sultans . . . [who] introduced many innovations in Indian music [and] also said to have invented the *sitar*'.[77]

What is exceptional in these examples of cultural history from the Mughal period is that despite centuries of warfare, a unique idea of Indo-Islamic culture emerged during this time. It was shaped by a host of reasons and circumstances, but what is distinct is the emergence of innovations in taste that ranged from food to clothing and also in aesthetic forms like music and literature. Language is more fundamental than religion, and cultural conversions occur through the various forms of language.

The relationship between India and Hinduism is mediated by a history that includes the intervention of other faiths, such as Buddhism, Jainism, Islam and Christianity. All these religions came to acquire a distinctive identity within India's geo-cultural boundary and in the process brought in changes within Hinduism itself. Changes come from the 'synthesis' which Nehru traces right back to the meeting between the Aryans and the Dravidians, and later between the settlers and the Iranians, Greeks, Parthians, Bactrians, Scythians, Huns, Turks (before Islam), early Christians, Jews (and) Zoroastrians.

Nehru marvels at how despite 'caste and exclusiveness', India retains an 'astonishing inclusive capacity'[78]. For Weber, 'the assimilative power of the Hindu life order' precisely comes from 'its legitimation of social rank, and, not to be forgotten, possible related economic advantages'.[79] Weber does also acknowledge that 'Hinduism is unusually tolerant of doctrine (*mata*)'.[80]

Nehru locates the idea of culture outside the prism of caste and doctrine, and understands Hinduism only in the 'widest sense of Indian culture'.[81] Hinduism represents a culture more than a religion, and Nehru is one of the sole Indian nationalists of the era to have made this distinction by offering historical reasons.[82] Nehru's idea of tradition is also contextual: every tradition has its own 'spirit' of historical evolution.

'[There] is a special heritage for us in India' he writes in *The Discovery*, yet 'not an exclusive one, for none is exclusive and all are common to the race of man'.[83] Here Nehru does hint at a universality of thought and culture, though premised upon heterogeneity of cultures.

Octavio Paz has noted how, in the context of British colonialism in India, Nehru 'saw the opposition between East and West as the clash between two historical realities'.[84] Paz understood that 'for Nehru, the clash between different cultures was rather fictitious; the real thing was the historical opposition'.[85] What does this distinction between culture and history signify?

Culture is the open site of intellectual and artistic life of the community. It is porous and always liable to influences. History is the name of time whose nature is paradoxical. It is both singular or specific and diversely (or, heterogeneously) universal. History tells you of the stage of collective life that determines the difference between cultures. Even though culture is an integral—and intimate—part of history, it has different characteristics, and behaves differently, vis-à-vis history.

Caution is necessary to not slip into a linear idea of history that is determined by ideas of progress. To have one scale to measure the varying stages of cultures is the modernist arrogance of Enlightenment and post-Enlightenment thought. The world has witnessed the progress of European barbarism in Africa and Asia throughout modernity. No one denies the brilliance of European thought and literature and the beauty of their art. No one denies the ethical force in the ideas of *liberty, equality and fraternity* proclaimed as the ideals of the French Revolution in the late eighteenth century. Despite these ideas, however, Europe gifted Auschwitz and the Gulags to its own people that it did not consider its own, and hence, not fit to live. It gifted itself war. It plundered and humiliated Africa and Asia with colonialism and slavery. The idea of progress propagated by the intellectual castle of European thought is the most defining and tragic lie of modernity.

Nehru raises the question of identity that is modern, but one that does not come from the *sole* premises of Enlightenment rationality. It comes from a Romantic sense of individuality where a person belongs both inside and outside of one's culture. It comes from a lived experience of cultural heterogeneity, which is not simply an issue about critical engagement with one's tradition. It is also part of Romanticism, but from recognition of a more diverse cultural history.

Paz's overstates the point on Nehru's universalist stance:

> Contrary to the anthropologists and the historians who postulate the multiplicity of cultures, Nehru affirmed the unity of thought and the universality of science, art and technology. In this universality, he saw the answer to the antagonism of the historical worlds.[86]

One cannot entirely agree with this observation. It is true that Nehru believed in the coming of a modern culture that he wished would replace traditional cultures completely. And there is bound to be a tendency towards homogeneity when science and technology become part of everyday culture. Nehru did not envisage that modern culture would become the *same* in every country. He wouldn't have been arguing over so many pages in *The Discovery* over India's unique cultural identity if he didn't believe simultaneously in cultural heterogeneity, even if it is understood within the bounds of (and problems posed by) national culture. The paradox that connects cultural specificity to cultural heterogeneity is essential to the argument.

The universality of reason, both within the culture of science and technology as well as a wider intellectual bent towards objectivist knowledge, does tend to structure cultural specificities. Nehru understands the cultural capacity for synthesis as a normative. The normative merely lies in the evident nature of synthesis. The deeper cause of this synthesis comes from the attitude to look for meanings across cultures. It is the attitude of a free spirit, who is not necessarily a rationalist. We have seen that free spirit in pre-modern eras in travellers like Hiuen-Tsang, Al Biruni and Ibn Batuta. There are similar wanderers (and assimilators) of cultural knowledge. Nehru, however, exercises caution in plunging into a shallow attempt at synthesis that has been quite the case of India's intellectual elites:

> It should be equally obvious that there can be no cultural or spiritual growth based on imitation. Such imitation can only be confined to a small number which cuts itself off from the masses and the springs of national life. True culture derives its inspiration from every corner of the world but it is *home-grown* and has to be based on the *wide mass of the people* . . . The day of a narrow culture confined to a small fastidious group is past.[87]

Nehru, the Cultural Democrat

This idea separates Nehru from both the left and liberal variety of intellectuals in India. Nehru is a political thinker with a good measure of originality. He could see how ideological thought often created superficial rejections of cultural specificities. It happened among colonized intellectuals who were overwhelmed by the claims of scientific rationality and its universalizing norms. These intellectuals wanted to reject their own cultures as a baggage of the past, which they began to understand and analyse only in terms of political economy. The beliefs and values of pre-modern cultures were weighed against European modernism, and even more narrowly against socialist realism. Nehru bluntly aired his discomfort with Indian communists:

> I know that in India the Communist Party is completely divorced from, and is ignorant of, the national traditions that fill the minds of the people. It believes that communism necessarily implies a contempt for the past. So far as it is concerned, the history of the world began in November, 1917, and everything that preceded this was preparatory and leading up to it. Normally speaking, in a country like India with large numbers of people on the verge of starvation and the economic structure cracking up, communism should have a wide appeal. In a sense there is that vague appeal, but the Communist Party cannot take advantage of it because it has cut itself off from the springs of national sentiment and speaks in a language which finds no echo in the hearts of the people. It remains an energetic, but small group, with no real roots.[88]

This warning by Nehru was not heeded by a large number of Marxist intellectuals and scholars in India. The Russian Revolution was an exceptional political event that held the promise of radical equality and a challenge to world capitalism. But in a wrong demonstration of intellectual ethics, Marxists refused to acknowledge (and condemn) the violence and lies of Soviet communism under Stalin, and even after him. A singular lens of historical materialism was used to understand Indian history and culture. The *points of difference* between India and Europe were suppressed under the linear idea of progress. Culture was seen only through the prism of feudalism (as an exploitative economic structure) and religion (as a 'backward' and 'reactionary' belief system that aided feudalism).

Once a culture is put to test against a universal norm fixed by the standards set by another culture, the idea of heterogeneity is destroyed. Nehru himself, as we have seen, was prey to this problem. But since he was less doctrinaire than others, he could also raise doubts against himself. This is a rare quality in Nehru that is barely visible in other political thinkers of his time, or also in Indian intellectuals and scholars after him. The problem of modern ideology is based on the arrogant certainty of rationalist knowledge that simultaneously prevents self-doubt. Having used strong words against the penchant of communists in India to dismiss their own cultural heritage, Nehru still considers them better than liberals and other variants of Indian modernists who equally miss the point about valorizing European culture as an elitist fetish:

It is not only the Communist Party in India that has failed in this respect. There are others who talk glibly of modernism and modern spirit and the essence of western culture, and are at the same time ignorant of their own culture. Unlike the communists, they have no ideal that moves them and no driving force that carries them forward. They take the external forms and outer trappings of the west (and often some of the less desirable features), and imagine that they are in the vanguard of an advancing civilization. Naive and shallow and yet full of their own conceits, they live, chiefly in a few large cities, an artificial life which has no living contacts with the culture of the east or of the west.[89]

The civilizational vanguard, Nehru suggests, is much worse than vanguards of ideology. These 'others' appear to be elite liberals who imbibe the culture of modernity in their lifestyles and social etiquettes, but are not committed to what Nehru considers the genuine values of modernity. They lack the social and political ideals that move the modern spirit towards demanding change. Liberals, in Nehru's understanding, are the fake vanguards of modernity.

Partha Chatterjee noted how Nehru 'offers a direct rebuttal of the essentialist dichotomy between Eastern and Western cultures'.[90] He quotes this passage from *The Discovery* to establish his point:

> I do not understand the use of the words Orient and Occident, except in the sense that Europe and America are highly industrialized and Asia is backward in this respect. This industrialization is something new in the world's history . . . There is no organic connection between Hellenic civilization and modern European and American civilization.[91]

Nehru's lens of drawing the historical difference between the East and the West in terms of 'industrialization and lack of industrialization'[92] corroborates Paz's view. The difference between East and West is removed from the essentialist traps of colonialist perception and made historically contingent. Chatterjee concludes that with Nehru, 'nationalist thought has come to grips with the Orientalist thematic; . . . is now able to criticize it . . . has got rid of those cultural essentialisms that had confined it since birth and, at last, it is able to look at the histories of the nation and the world in their true specificities'.[93] Chatterjee, however, finds Nehru forwarding the argument that 'we must learn the material skills from the West without losing our spiritual heritage'.[94] This echoes Chatterjee's own view of the absurdist binary of the outer and inner, or material and spiritual domains that was supposedly produced within the anti-colonial self. In this regard, Chatterjee draws our attention to the following passage from *The Discovery*:

India, as well as China, must learn from the West, for the modern West has much to teach, and the spirit of the age is represented by the West. But the West is also obviously in need of learning much, and its advances in technology will bring it little comfort if it does not learn some of the deeper lessons of life, which have absorbed the minds of thinkers in all ages and in all countries.[95]

This doesn't seem to corroborate Chatterjee's binary. Nehru's point is that India's intellectual contribution to the colonial encounter is its synthetic idea of knowledge. Chatterjee further discovers Nehru asserting that 'ancient Indian thought was much closer to the spirit of the scientific attitude than the overall cultural values of the modern West'.[96] To establish the point, he quotes Nehru from *The Discovery*:

Science has dominated the Western world and everyone there pays tribute to it, and yet the West is still far from having developed the real temper of science. It has still to bring the spirit and the flesh into creative harmony . . . the essential basis of Indian thought for ages past, though not its later manifestations, fits in with the scientific temper and approach, as well as with internationalism. It is based on a fearless search for truth, on the solidarity of man, even on the divinity of everything living, and on the free and co-operative development of the individual and the species, ever to greater freedom and higher stages of human growth.[97]

Nehru relates the common ground of scientific knowledge to the 'fearless search for truth'. He finds India's cultural history even more suited to pursue the path of rationalist truth-seeking than the West. It is interesting that a divine vision of life is incorporated as a positive attribute to the spirit of truth-seeking in Indian culture.

In his bid to retain the Platonic ideal of 'integrated personalities',[98] Nehru often joins the categories that he otherwise holds apart. He is alert to realize the limits of specialized knowledge and work in the light of what he came to admire as the 'synthetic view of human life'[99] in India's cultural history. It made him doubt the idea of progress and emphasize the need for harmony.[100]

Nehru overcame the problem of binary posed by Orientalism. He doesn't find a quarrel happening between science and religion in Indian culture like it did in the West. For Nehru, 'scientific temper' means 'a way of life, a process of thinking, a method of acting and associating with our fellowmen . . . It is the temper of a free man'.[101]

It is a *democratic* ideal to which Nehru relates the scientific temper, the way he related the democratic idea with the issue of a genuine cultural synthesis, as was shown above. He finds the West wanting on the *ethical* and *moral* side of this critical temper, which he equates with the 'solidarity of man', 'free and co-operative development . . .' and 'greater freedom'. These are the views of a cultural democrat.

It is Nehru's commitment to the idea of democracy that is often ignored by Marxist critics. Chatterjee, for instance, finds Nehru's use of Marxism a case of 'selective appropriation' that harps on the 'rational and egalitarian side' while leaving out the 'political core'.[102] Professor of Politics, Sanjay Seth asserts that Nehru's thought, rather than being an appropriation, was 'consistent and coherent in its use of Marxism' and yet—Seth sharply proposes—it *equally consistently and coherently* yielded a non-Marxist politics'.[103] Seth feels that '[in] the colonies, where Marxism was not a critique of modernity, and where it was largely shorn of a distinctive political core'[104] the appropriation of Marxism was productive rather than limiting. Nehru's anti-colonial nationalism grappled with the paradox of adopting a critical stance vis-à-vis Western modernity, even as it welcomed the liberating principles of that modernity.

I would like to place the non-Marxist side of Nehru's politics to his understanding of what politics means in a democracy. In the *Azad Memorial Lectures* that he delivered in 1959, Nehru spoke with clarity on the subject:

> Marx was primarily moved by the ghastly conditions that prevailed in the early days of industrialization in Western Europe. At that time there was no truly democratic structure of the state, and changes could hardly be made constitutionally. Hence, revolutionary violence offered the only way to change. Marxism therefore, inevitably thought in terms of a violent revolution. Since then, however, political democracy has spread bringing with it the possibility of peaceful change . . . The democratic structure of the state, organized labour and, above all, the urge for social justice as well as scientific and technological progress, have brought about this transformation.[105]

Nehru's commitment to democracy is fundamental and sincere. He does not believe in the Marxist assumption that bourgeois democracy is a 'deceptive institutional arrangement'.[106] The optimism regarding science is equally persistent in Nehru. In *The Discovery*, Nehru distinguishes between what he means by 'science' and contrasts it with 'scientific temper' that he believes the West lacks in relation to India:

Science deals with the domain of positive knowledge but the *temper* which it should produce *goes beyond* that domain. The ultimate purposes of man may be said to be to gain knowledge, to realize truth, to appreciate goodness and beauty. The scientific method of objective enquiry is *not* applicable to all these, and much that is vital in life seems to lie *beyond its scope* – the sensitiveness of art and poetry, the emotion that beauty produces, the inner recognition of goodness.[107]

Nehru at times *specifically* points out why he prefers the need for objectivity against exclusionary practices both ritual and social in nature: science:

India must lessen her religiosity and turn to science. She must get rid of the exclusiveness in thought and social habit which has made life a prison for her, stunning her spirit and preventing growth. The idea of *ceremonial purity* has erected barriers against social intercourse and narrowed the sphere of social action. The day-to-day religion of the orthodox Hindu is more concerned with what to eat and what not to eat, who to eat with and from whom to keep away, than with *spiritual values*. The rules and regulations of the kitchen dominate his social life.[108]

Though there is a constant 'tension' in Nehru between an optimistic attitude towards science and a more cautious regard for cultural traditions, it is of course true that Nehru tilted towards pro-scientific progress. He was always vehemently opposed to what he called 'that narrowing religious outlook . . . that obsession with the supernatural and metaphysical speculations, that loosening of the mind's discipline in religious ceremonial and mystical emotionalism'.[109] In fact, Nehru advised that even when 'realizing . . . (the) limitations of reason and scientific method, we have still to hold on to them with all our strength, for without that firm basis and background we can have no grip on *any* kind of truth or reality'.[110] Reason is the new basis for evaluating truth.

The New Woman

Nehru's understanding of the cultural question includes his sensitive views regarding women. Writing *The Discovery* in the Ahmednagar Fort prison, Nehru is aware of the history of the brave woman whose story reverberates in the walls of the fort-turned-prison:

> [This] is a place of history, of many a battle and palace intrigue in the past. That history is not very old, as Indian history goes, nor is it very important in the larger scheme of things. But one incident stands out and is still remembered: the courage of a beautiful woman, Chand Bibi, who defended this fort and led her forces, sword in hand, against the imperial armies of Akbar. She was murdered by one of her own men.[111]

This reference to Chand Bibi, the sixteenth-century ruler of the Ahmednagar Sultanate (in the region of Maharashtra), is a short but poignant mention of a brave woman warrior from medieval history. This piece of history is too small to be regarded as part of the larger story of national history, and yet the 'incident stands out': the 'courage of a beautiful woman' who defended her fort against Akbar was no ordinary woman. Nehru, himself involved in the ambitious task of writing a grand history of India, pauses to pay his tribute to an exemplary (but historically minor) character of courage. The tone and sentiment is similar when Nehru describes the Revolt of 1857. After acknowledging the guerilla

leaders including the 'brilliant . . . Tantia Topi',[112] Nehru comes
to the most important figure of the mutiny:

> One name stands out above others and is revered still in
> popular memory, the name of Lakshmi Bai, Rani of Jhansi, a
> girl of twenty years of age, who died fighting. 'Best and bravest'
> of the rebel leaders, she was called by the English general who
> opposed her.[113]

Once again Nehru pauses to mention a minor but well-known figure
that appears in our history textbooks, and in that famous eulogy
by the Hindi poet Ramdhari Singh Dinkar. Nehru pays tribute to
the ruler of Jhansi for standing up to the British. It is noteworthy
that though Lakshmi Bai (unlike Chand Bibi) is a glorified figure
of the Indian woman warrior queen, in the context of the modern
folklore of nationalism, Nehru does not exaggerate or romanticize
her. He simply says—she was 'above others', who were all men. The
compliment by a British general is the last word on her reputation.
   In a striking paragraph Nehru lays down the larger view of
women in India down the ages:

> Indian history is full of the names of famous women, including
> thinkers and philosophers, rulers and warriors. This freedom
> grew progressively less. Islam had a fairer law of inheritance
> but this did not affect Hindu women. What did affect many of
> them to their great disadvantage, as it affected Moslem women
> to a much greater degree, was the intensification of the custom
> of seclusion of women. This spread among the upper classes all
> over the north and in Bengal, but the south and west of India
> escaped this degrading custom. Even in the north, only the
> upper classes indulged in it and the masses were happily free
> from it. Women now had less chances of education and their

activities were largely confined to the household. Lacking most other ways of distinguishing themselves, living a confined and restricted life, they were told that their supreme virtue lay in chastity and the supreme sin in a loss of it. Such was the man-made doctrine, but man did not apply it to himself.[114]

The law of inheritance in Muslim society was more equitable regarding women compared to Hindu society. Nehru mentions, referring to Manu, that the 'legal position of [Hindu] women . . . were always dependent on somebody—on the father, the husband, or the son . . . they were treated, in law, as chattels'.[115] He adds, however, with a touch of comparative history, that even though the legal status of Hindu woman in ancient times was poor, 'it was far better than in ancient Greece and Rome, in early Christianity, in the Canon Law of mediaeval Europe, and indeed right up to comparatively modern times at the beginning of the nineteenth century'.[116]

Nehru found the purdah system that forced Muslim women to stay indoors as a negative cultural influence, and felt it had a bad impact on the lives of Hindu women. Nehru, however, does not offer any explanation why the privileged class/caste among Hindus came to imbibe this practice of seclusion. Historically, the purdah system was adopted by Muslims after the Arab conquest of Iraq in the seventh century ad.[117] The practice, apart from restrictions to freedom and mobility, also prevented women from acquiring education. Oppressive moral codes were used to regulate the mind and behaviour of women who were forced under a mechanism of double control: being controlled by men as well as inventing modes of self-control.

Nehru brings up the question of women early in *The Discovery* with a fine touch of modern sensibility when talking about his wife, Kamala:

She wanted to play her own part in the national struggle and not be merely a hanger-on and a shadow of her husband. She wanted to justify herself to her own self as well as to the world. Nothing in the world could have pleased me more than this, but I was far too busy to see beneath the surface, and I was blind to what she looked for and so ardently desired. And then prison claimed me so often and I was away from her, or else she was ill. Like Chitra in Tagore's play, she seemed to say to me: 'I am Chitra. No goddess to be worshipped, nor yet the object of common pity to be brushed aside like a moth with indifference. If you deign to keep me by your side in the path of danger and daring, if you allow me to share the great duties of your life, then you will know my true self'.[118]

For a woman, to be part of the anti-colonial movement meant seeking her own self-justification, as well as her own place in the world. It is finding the ground of one's own meaning. The field of nationalist struggle was for most Indian thinkers and activists, a means and occasion to define the self in relation to a new ground for freedom. To realize this Kamala had to become her own person, her own woman. One can only fight for a larger cause of freedom that one experiences within the self. Nehru switches to the mode of dramatic monologue by making a character from Tagore's play, personify his wife. The monologue offers Tagore's vision of the new woman who refuses to be trapped in the image of divinity, or be treated as an object of neglect and sympathy. She is willing to take the same risks as a man, to find her feet in the world. The question of facing danger together demolishes the gendered nature of difference between man and woman that creates a division of labour, offering them different roles to fulfil their own nature, and place assigned in society. Men and women are equal and different, where difference is not essentialized using gendered norms. A woman's desire to experience the same *political* danger as a man is both a demand for equality and an assertion of a different subjectivity. A man and a woman come from different experiences of life, and different histories to address, critique and to overcome. Even if they risk *the same thing* they risk it *differently*. The experience of equality allows the free experience of difference, a woman's 'true self'.

Nehru goes ahead to offer a panoramic view of how women's presence and participation in the national movement added to its force. Speaking about the political situation in the early 1930s, Nehru writes:

> Most of us menfolk were in prison. And then a remarkable thing happened. Our women came to the front and took charge of the struggle. Women had always been there of course, but now there was an avalanche of them, which took not only the British Government but their own menfolk by surprise. Here were these women, women of the upper or middle classes, leading sheltered lives in their homes—peasant women, working class women, rich women—pouring out in their tens of thousands in defiance of government order and police lathi. It was not only that display of courage and daring, but what was even more surprising was the organizational power they showed.[119]

It is a revolutionary moment for women to enter the field of the anti-colonial movement when the men were absent. This unique circumstance allowed the women to occupy centre stage. Sociologist Suruchi Thapar has written on the time 'when the nationalist leadership were in gaol, the women took over the leadership roles and provided guidance to the movement'.[120] Thapar mentions that the 'forms of agitation involved leading processions, holding meetings and courting arrest'.[121] She writes on the construction of the 'new woman' that emerged from the nationalist discourse since the nineteenth century, where women's roles centred on questions of education and moral norms of behaviour,[122] to the twentieth century, where Gandhi joined the anticolonial movement in the 1920s and encouraged women's participation in the political sphere. The Gandhian code of representation associated women with 'self-sacrifice', 'silent suffering' and 'self-reliance'.[123]

Nehru saw women as open and free political subjects who could face danger and be equal to men.

4

History and the 'Roots of the Present'

In the *Azad Memorial Lectures* in 1959, Nehru said that the historical moment he was in was one of 'tumult' and 'confusion', where 'we stand facing both ways, forward towards the future and backwards towards the past, being pulled in two directions'.[1]

Nehru grappled with this paradoxical nature of time in modernity, ever since the days of writing *Glimpses of World History* in 1934 and more than ten year later in 1946, in *The Discovery of India*. How to reconcile the historical past and the present was his lifelong intellectual preoccupation.

Nehru delves into the question of past and present early in *The Discovery*:

The roots of [the] present lay in the past and so I made voyages of discovery into the past, ever seeking a clue in it, if any such existed, to the understanding of the present. The domination of the present never left me even when I lost myself in musings of past, events and of persons far away and long ago, forgetting where or what I was. If I felt occasionally that I belonged to the past. I felt also that the whole of the past belonged to me in the present. Past history merged into contemporary history: it became a living reality tied up with sensations of pain and pleasure. If the past had a tendency to become the present, the present also sometimes receded into the distant past and assumed its immobile, statuesque appearance. In the midst of an intensity of action itself, there would suddenly come a feeling as if it was some past event and one was looking at it, as it were, in retrospect.[2]

The first striking aspect of this passage is that Nehru is simultaneously talking about the larger time of history, as well as how he is himself situated in this criss-cross between the past and present. Time is not simply out there, to be understood objectively. Time is also within, to be felt as a subjective experience. This time is historical time, and it is felt both inside and outside. Time is about design and association, structure and feeling. There is generality and specificity about historical time. It is an idea of history that includes both events and the internality of the subject of history. Nehru understands the experiential time of history as something that is able to freeze the passing moment into an image of history. Charles Baudelaire famously described time in modernity as, 'the transient, the fleeting, the contingent'.[3] The historian's task is to be able to frame this fleeting and contingent moment. In Nehru's case the historian is also, uniquely, someone who experiences the passing of history in the middle of intense action. Nehru explains this intensity in terms of political activity as a participant in the anti-colonial movement. He writes, how 'the call of action stirs strange depths within me . . . I want to experience again "that lonely impulse of delight", which turns to risk and danger and faces and mocks at death'.[4] To turn the moment of danger into a moment of action and seize upon it to find meaning is the source of Nehru's relationship with politics and history. The secret of time and time of history is to pay attention to this fleeting moment where you risk your being, your life, for something that stirs you. History begins, is realized and is stored in the secret of that moment. Of course, there is a historical past that one is born into and one reads about. Nehru seeks clues from history to understand the present. Finally, it is through the subject of history that past is made present, and they collapse in the moment of action. For Nehru, the present dominated over the past. It was only *as* present that the past revealed itself to him, just as *through* the present he could belong to the past.

Nehru underlines this idea of belonging to history:

> Because my own personal experiences have often touched historic events . . . it has not been difficult for me to envisage history as a living process with which I could identify myself to some extent. I came late to history and, even then, not through the usual direct road of learning a mass of facts and dates and drawing conclusions and inferences from them, unrelated to my life's course. So long as I did this, history had little significance for me.[5]

Nehru 'touched' historical events. The event is not simply outside him, demanding pure objectivity. He is part of the event, and that allows the feeling of a 'living' relationship with history.

Latecomer to History

It is only in modernity that a man could say, 'I came late to history'.

The statement isn't simply about a sense of distance from the beginning of dated history. It is about the knowledge of history. The voluminous industry of history writing that tells you about how far back in time you could go, and how vast the corpus of events are, makes you feel enough has happened in the world through the centuries before you. The coming late into history also suggests a burden, of being saddled with a lot of baggage, of having to relate to it and evaluate one's relationship with it. Nehru as a man and a keen student of history, feels that the present is under an obligation to the past that it cannot shrug off. He writes: 'The burden of the past, the burden of both good and ill, is over-powering, and sometimes suffocating, more especially for those of us who belong to a very ancient civilization.'[6]

Keeping Hegel in mind, Nietzsche finds 'the belief that one is a latecomer in the world . . . harmful and degrading'.[7] The modern latecomer of the Hegelian kind believes in the conceit, according to Nietzsche, where history replaces everything else as the only sovereign power of universal proportions—'God's sojourn upon earth'[8]—and the philosopher of history himself, à la Hegel, being the centre of this highest state of existence.

Nehru, in contrast, is a latecomer who is reeling from the burden of history. He is looking for clues to negotiate between history and politics. He is not trying to theorize a law of history, rather formulate an attitude towards it. Nehru is far from a Hegelian conviction that he is at the highest stage of history. Indian history has come a way long since ancient times and presents us with the challenge of belonging. Nehru was interested in history both as a chronicler and participant. He saw a certain relationship between the two. Nehru contemplates the historical roots of human action: 'Any vital action springs from the depths of the being. All the long past of the individual and even of the race has prepared the background for that psychological moment of action.'[9]

Nehru is quite aware of the past weighing heavily on him He did not believe in 'absolute determinism', but also considered that the 'apparent exercise of free will, is itself conditioned'.[10] History was difficult to get out of. These considerations are important for a man who set out to make and change history. There is a complex chain that Nehru builds between past and present which is not just unique to Nehru, but also unique to what Nehru marks as a fundamental difference between India and the West. His views reflect the *pragmatic* kind of what Hegel called 'reflective history',[11] where conditions of the present inform one's situation and judgement. However, thanks to his Nietzschean doubts, Nehru does not follow the Hegelian guidelines for a 'world history'[12] based on reason alone. Nehru grants historical importance to India's epics,[13] Ashokan edicts and Akbar's attempts at synthesizing religious thought as evidence of a political culture from which we can gain historical knowledge. For Hegel, 'India's epic poems have no historical foundation',[14] and 'the law of history doesn't apply to India'[15] as there is no empirical evidence of a 'law of succession'[16] of sovereignty that runs through the ages. India's disqualification from Hegelian world history and its Western rationality proves that neither can this idea of history claim the world, nor is the world definable by Western criteria.

Reading Michel de Certeau, Sanjay Seth discovers that the French scholar's idea of history implies that *'the past of non-Western countries is not history's past'*.[17] It did not occur to de Certeau that if the non-West can't be fitted into a Western idea of history, it is the latter that needs to question and broaden its perception. Western historicism needs to shrug off its Hegelian trappings. It is not that the non-West lacks (*this*) history, but that (*this*) history lacks the non-West.

Partha Chatterjee restricts his focus on Nehru's rebuttal of the Orientalist discourse of European colonialist knowledge that essentialized the East as backward, religious and superstitious, against the West that they considered rational and progressive. Nehru indeed questioned the 'unread crowd' that believed in the 'essential difference between the east and the west'.[18] He compared ancient India and Greece, holding that both civilizations had 'the same broad, tolerant, pagan outlook, joy in life and in the surprising beauty and infinite variety of nature, love of art'.[19] He cut through the cultural essentialisms to admit that the West was ahead in industrialization—and that was all there is to East being East, and West being West.

But the most interesting paradox that Nehru laid out regarding India facing the past and the present (and the past *in* the present), which frames the East–West discourse, is regarding 'continuity'. The idea of continuity has a huge bearing on Nehru's idea of history and modernity. It creates the perfect narrative of a cultural paradox that defines the abiding predicament of modern India better than anything else.

In the following passage, we find Nehru grappling with delightful vacillations in his mind and in language, trying to find his way out of a dilemma:

> India must break with much of her past and not allow it to dominate the present. Our lives are encumbered with the dead wood of the past . . . But that does not mean a break with, or a forgetting of, the vital and life giving in that past.
>
> We can never forget the ideals that have moved . . . the wisdom of the ancients . . . the daring of their thought, their splendid achievements in literature, art and culture, their love of truth and beauty and freedom . . . their toleration of other ways than theirs, their capacity to absorb other peoples and their cultural accomplishments, to synthesize them and develop a varied and mixed culture . . . If India forgets them she will no

longer remain India and much that has made her our joy and pride will cease to be.[20]

The past is not *just one thing* for Nehru.

The past is the 'dead wood' of habits and customs that must go—'caste' and the decay of '[ideas] of truth, beauty and freedom' and people becoming 'prisoners following a deadening routine'.[21]

Nehru's verdict was straight: 'Indian civilization went to seed because it became static, self-absorbed and inclined to narcissism.'[22]

This view echoes what Octavio Paz, who studied India deeply, wrote on what went wrong between the sixth and thirteenth centuries BCE:

> There was no 'reconstitution' [referring to the term used by Alfred Kroeber], only repetition, mannerism, self-imitation, and finally, sclerosis. It was not the invasions of white Huns that put an end to Indian civilization but that civilization's inability to reconstruct itself or fecundate itself.[23]

And yet, Nehru's argument seems to be that decay doesn't mean that some of those values of the past should be made redundant. In cultural terms, tolerance and synthesis are two values that served India well. Even though a break from the past, like it happened in the West, must also take place in Indian modernity—it cannot be a *complete* break. And this is the crucial Nehruvian turn in historical terms, where history is not merely the story of events but the value and spirit that we retrieve from them. Nehru felt overwhelmed by what he felt was 'unique about the continuity of a cultural tradition through five thousand years of history, of invasion and upheaval, a tradition which was widespread among the masses and powerfully influenced them'.[24]

In a striking passage, Nehru integrates the idea of 'progress' with the idea of continuity, and gives a whole new Indian twist to what the West hailed as an idea that necessarily entails a complete break with the economy of a feudal and religious past:

> National progress can, therefore, neither lie in a repetition of the past nor in its denial. New patterns must inevitably be adopted but they must be integrated with the old . . . Indian history is a striking record of changes introduced in this way, a continuous adaptation of old ideas to a changing environment, of old patterns to new. Because of this there is no sense of cultural break in it and there is that *continuity*, in spite of repeated change, from the far distant days of Mohenjodaro to our own age.[25]

Progress—the central idea behind social and political change and freedom since the beginning of the nineteenth century, envisaged by liberals and Marxists alike, was directly related to scientific knowledge and advance, and what was believed to be the liberating power of reason. Progress was also a road to the mastery of the self, and of (human) nature. Modernity was a project of inventing the 'new man' of science, rationality and progress. This new historical specimen was supposed to get rid of the past and become a being of pure present, like a laboratory product.

Nehru never takes that Enlightenment line, despite championing the necessity of scientific temperament and reason. There is a hesitation and doubt in Nehru that repeatedly sneaks in regarding the promise of progress. It is not simply an intuitive hesitation or doubt, but also historical. Finding a lack of 'poise' in the West that 'progressed so much in other directions', Nehru wonders if 'it should be possible to have a union of poise and inner and outer progress, of the wisdom of the old with the science and the vigour of the new'.[26]

On another note, Nehru could also see that Western culture and society also faced a cultural crisis:

> It would seem that the kind of modern civilization that developed first in the west and spread elsewhere, and especially the metropolitan life that has been its chief feature, produces an unstable society which gradually loses its vitality. Life advances in many fields and yet it loses its grip; it becomes more artificial and slowly ebbs away. More and more stimulants are needed— drugs to enable us to sleep or to perform our other natural functions, foods and drinks that tickle the palate and produce a momentary exhilaration at the cost of weakening the system, and special devices to give us a temporary sensation of pleasure and excitement—and after the stimulation comes the reaction and a sense of emptiness.[27]

This is a striking passage on the artifice of urban life, where Nehru sharply describes how mass consumption of stimulants consumed to drive away a sense of emptiness, ends up intensifying it. He does not succumb to any moral judgement in this regard but suggests a spiritual loneliness of the individual.

Nehru's profound concerns on modernity's impact on culture are also strikingly Weberian. The German thinker had moments of pessimism on whether science and rationalization were leading modern society necessarily towards a liberating end. In an essay titled, 'Religious Rejections of the World and their Directions', Weber registers his doubts:

> [Science] in the name of 'intellectual integrity', has come forward with the claim of representing the only possible form

of reasoned view of the word . . . The advancement of cultural values, however, seems to become a senseless hustle in the service of worthless, moreover self-contradictory, and mutually antagonistic ends.[28]

Weber is aware that scientific rationality has produced contradictions in cultural life, where rational certainties have ended in confusion and meaninglessness.

Nehru asks a deeper question of modernity:

What is wrong with modern civilization which produces at the roots these signs . . . Is there a cycle governing this inner decay and can we seek out the causes and eliminate them? Modern industrialism and the capitalist structure of society cannot be the sole causes, for decadence has often occurred without them.[29]

Beneath the crisis of industrialism and capitalism, Nehru detects a deeper hole in the heart of modernity. The other side of progress is a dungeon of despair. That is where Nehru falls back upon the need for continuity. He does not want India to reach and experience the dead ends of modernity that he could see in the West. Nehru's answer to the West's proclamation of absolute newness heralded by science, reason and progress is '[new] patterns', where the past and the present can exist in a new form. Modernity introduced a new pattern to life and culture—to the way we understood social relations, political ideals, and history itself.

On rare occasions, Nehru illuminates the idea of holding on to the past and looking for signs of continuity in specific terms. He gives us a glimpse of the picture, which is different from Gandhian cultural tropes like the Ram Rajya.

In *Glimpses of World History*, Nehru writes in the section—'The Lesson of History', how he often undergoes a visual experience of the historical past, which helps him relate to the present moment. He calls them 'ill-arranged images, like a gallery with no order in the arrangement of pictures'.[30] This haphazard row of images defies the chronology of time. Historical imagination or memory is not linear. It makes its own sequence, depending on one's own subjective drive or association. The sequence of events is arranged subjectively to extract, what Nehru calls, 'a lesson in them for my guidance'.[31] Defining history as a 'growth from barbarism to civilization',[32] Nehru sometimes finds that 'past periods of history . . . seem to be better than ours'.[33] It makes him wonder if the world 'is going forward or backward'.[34] It is a judgement against the dominant strand of Western political thought. The idea of modern history as a story of progress is put under doubt.

Nehru shares further in the same book, his excitement about people in his time being 'in the direct line . . . with the ancients, who came down through the north-western mountain passes into the smiling planes of what was to be known as Brahmavarta and Aryavarta and Bharatvarsha and Hindustan'.[35] There cannot be a more emphatic illustration of enthusiasm for the past of ancestral strangers. The different names of India have significance by the changing nature of their meanings. The 'direct line' that connects past and present once again marks the intense sense of continuity that Nehru feels is in the nature of our historical time. To be connected to one's past and be able to retrieve it at will, is a luxury that Nehru wouldn't like to give up.

The idea of historical time in Nehru seems to exist in two planes simultaneously: inside and the outside, the imagined and the existent. History must ultimately speak through the subject.

The third illustration that Nehru makes of our ties with the past is to attach significance to our cultural history (and memory), regarding religious festivals that lead pilgrims to the riverbanks of the Ganga and Yamuna. 'It is fascinating to think of the unbroken chain which connects us with the dim and distant past, to read accounts of these *melas* written 1300 years ago—and the *mela* was an old tradition even then.'[36] But ever alert to adding a necessary caution, Nehru adds, that 'we shall have to break through the prison of tradition whenever it prevents us from our onward march'.[37]

The most recent example is governmental reluctance to disturb the 'prison of tradition'. The April 2021 Kumbh Mela, in the middle of the rising second wave of the COVID-19 pandemic, created a health emergency due to the spreading of the virus. Lakhs of people took a dip in the waters to perform bathing rituals, reportedly violating norms set to tackle the spread of the pandemic.[38] If the lives of people are put under risk by allowing custom to disregard health protocols, it is not just a problem of lacking a secular will by appeasing the majority, but it is the intellectual failure to evaluate the meaning of tradition in relation to time and contingency. This is not about the past and present form of tradition, but the indifference and stupidity of modern politics. This is also not an argument of scientificity, where you accuse the government of succumbing to superstition. Culture is more complex than theoretical constructs that impose binaries of reason and unreason. Traditions need common sense when human lives are at stake. Beyond that, judgements based on (the demands of) rationality don't hold.

The late Colombian novelist Gabriel García Márquez was asked by Colombian journalist, Plinio Apuleyo Mendoza, to explain his own statement, 'If you don't believe in God, at least be superstitious.'[39] Márquez, who considered the matter serious, replied: 'I believe that superstitions, or what are commonly called such, correspond to natural forces which rational thinking, like that of the West, has rejected.'[40]

Most of India's liberal and left intellectuals fail to understand what Márquez calls 'natural forces' or life-forces that cannot be determined using a rational yardstick. These natural forces are particularly evident in times of natural calamities.

The sharpest caution that Nehru casts upon the idea of science as progress is when he firmly makes the point in *The Discovery*:

> The very progress of science, unconnected with and isolated from moral discipline and ethical considerations, will lead to the concentration of power and the terrible instruments of destruction which it has made, in the hands of evil and selfish men, seeking the domination of others—and thus to the destruction of its own great achievements.[41]

The politics of reason goes hand in hand with the moral ambiguity of the scientific temperament. The West is more than guilty of the destruction it caused to others and itself in modernity. Measured against this darkness, the claims to scientific achievement rings hollow[42].

Finally, let me address three observations that Nehru makes specifically in connection to Indian history. The first is Nehru's problem with the colonial writing of history:

> History is almost always written by the victors and conquerors and gives their viewpoint; or, at any rate, the victors' version is given prominence and holds the field. Very probably, all the early records we have of the Aryans in India, their epics and traditions, glorify the Aryans and are unfair to the people of the country whom they subdued. No individual can wholly rid himself of his racial outlook and cultural limitations, and when

there is conflict between races and countries even an attempt
at impartiality is considered a betrayal of one's people . . . The
overpowering need of the *moment* is to *justify* one's own actions
and condemn and blacken those of the enemy . . . In the old
days when war and its consequences, brutality and conquest
and enslavement of a people, were *accepted* as belonging to the
natural order of events, there was no particular need to cover
them or justify them from some other point of view. With the
growth of higher standards the need for *justification* has arisen,
and it leads to a perversion of facts, sometimes deliberate, often
unconscious.[43]

Earlier, in the pre-modern era, history was a natural event.
It happened and passed. There was no pedagogical mode of
representation that became part of institutional knowledge.
Western modernity and the logic of colonialism imposed
justifications on its actions. This was the beginning of professional
history writing. The unconscious is the cultural surplus of power
that seeks validation by any means. The discourse of justificatory
knowledge was a pedagogic mode of displaying Western
superiority over colonized subjects. Nationalist history was
caught by this initial challenge to refute the essentialist claims of
knowledge behind the justificatory logic of Western rule. It was
partly a reaction, and response to colonialism.

What Is *Not* History?

Next, Nehru turns his attention to nationalist historiography.
'Indians' he wrote, 'are peculiarly liable to accept tradition
and report as history, uncritically and without sufficient
examination'.[44] But 'the impact of science and the modern world
have brought a greater appreciation of facts, a more critical

faculty, a weighing of evidence, a refusal to accept tradition merely because it is tradition'.[45] However, Nehru is quick to point out that many 'competent historians . . . err on the *other side* and their work is more a meticulous chronicle of facts than living history'.[46] Nehru makes a clear distinction between tradition and history. History, unlike tradition, is not a matter of sentiments. It is objective and must bear the verdict of facts. It is not myth, hence evidence is necessary. The other side of the argument, however, is perhaps most crucial, particularly in India's context: *Tradition is not history.*

What does it mean, however, to 'report' tradition as history? Tradition can include oral culture, epics, folk customs and social structures and hierarchies. They involve beliefs and practices. What prevents traditions from being history? History is a discipline, or discourse, of weighing a certain fact or claim in time. All claims of tradition are put to the test of facts and evidences according to fixed dates or periods, and also movement or changes across time. One must establish a particular tradition qua tradition through this process of weighing facts and claims. Only then does tradition becomes history. Nehru is alluding to the tendency to pass off tradition as history, without a proper examination of its characteristics as well as its nature of existence over time. It must be pointed out that history does not have to be restricted to this pedagogic grid. An engagement with narratives of tradition can also bring us fruitful knowledge about how people thought and imaged at a certain point of time. Ancient and medieval texts offer us different versions of history. They can also be critically examined within a certain disciplinary rigour.

It is not just older traditions that require scrutiny. Modern traditions, like the writing of colonial history, as we have seen, distort history by planting justifications that are not based on facts but prejudice. Colonial rationality suffers from prejudice, where the modernist binary between reason and prejudice collapses.

Nehru points out to an abiding problem in Indian history that was initially introduced by British colonialist historians, but uncritically followed by Indian historians of the nationalist school later. Such are the unavoidable ironies of writing, history or any other thing, when you are under the intellectual influence of colonial power. Nehru writes:

> Indian history has usually been divided by English as well as some Indian historians into three major periods: Ancient or Hindu, Moslem, and the British period. This division is neither intelligent nor correct; it is deceptive and gives a wrong perspective. It deals more with the superficial changes at the top than with the essential changes in the political, economic, and cultural development of the Indian people. The so-called ancient period is vast and full of change, of growth and decay, and then growth again. What is called the Moslem or medieval period brought another change [but] did not vitally affect the essential continuity of Indian life. The invaders . . . became absorbed into India and part of her life . . . and there was a great deal of racial fusion by intermarriage . . . They looked to India as their home country and had no other affiliations . . . The British remained outsiders, aliens and misfits in India, and made no attempt to be otherwise. Above all, for the first time in India's history, her political control was exercised from outside and her economy was centered in a distant place. They made India a typical colony of the modern age, a subject country for the first time in her long history.[47]

The politics of periodization by colonial historians tried to recreate the European Middle Ages in India by painting the

Mughal period in a bad light. It also served the British policy of divide and rule. The historian, Brajadulal Chattopadhyay, mentions that this scheme of periodization of Indian history into 'Hindu' and 'Muslim' has contributed to 'marginalizing the continuity, interaction and modification of cultural elements in history'.[48]

Against the self-representation of the British as harbingers of Indian modernity and progress, Nehru, with his anti-colonial sensibility, does not hesitate to consider them 'outsiders, aliens and misfits' to India and its history. In contrast, Nehru treats the Muslims as an integral part of India's political and cultural life. We can compare this assertion by Nehru with what Tagore writes on the medieval encounter:

> We had known the hordes of Moghals and Pathans who invaded India . . . as human races, with their own religions and customs . . . we had never known them as a nation . . . we fought for them and against them, talked with them in a language which was theirs as well as our own.[49]

It is the politics of the nation as introduced by British colonizers that has created a real rupture in the history of India. Nationalism (and with it, nationalist history writing) has the unenviable task of countering both the logic of colonial history as well as remain critical of the dangers of nationalism. After all, nationalism is also inadvertently part of the same rupture caused by colonial history. To see nationalism only as a positive force against colonialism will make it difficult to address the question of the past. Be it the Hindu right or intellectuals and scholars belonging to other ideological persuasions, the irony that must be borne in mind is that any valorization of the nationalist discourse would lead to wrong impressions of the pre-modern past. The pre-colonial cannot retrospectively serve as an extension of the eulogies reserved for nationalist pride.

Against the factual and established idea of history, Nehru introduces the idea of 'living history', where the subject understands himself as (part of) history, and makes a reflective idea of history possible. This idea might be able to address what Benedict Anderson calls the 'philosophical poverty'[50] of nationalism.

What Nehru indicates by 'living history' is the emphasis of two elements into history writing: subjectivity and the larger question of ethics or values, or the idea of the good. The latter is not exactly an ideological demand, but it can be political. History written with an idea of progress in mind tends to read past and present events through a political lens. Modern history writing is political and hence a contested zone. Nehru's own attempt in *The Discovery*, to write a living history of his people, carries the mark of the modernist project of history as a discourse of representation.

I would like to end on a slightly different note by fusing the question of history with Nehru's own historical project of discovering India. In other words, I shall draw this discussion to a close by adhering to Nehru's idea, where the subject shall mark his vision upon the context that he is laying down for us.

The most exceptional moment in *The Discovery of India* is this passage near the end:

The discovery of India—what have I discovered? It was presumptuous of me to imagine that I could unveil her and find out what she is to-day and what she was in the long past. To-day she is four hundred million separate individual men and women, each differing from the other, each living in a private universe of thought and feeling. If this is so in the present, how much more difficult is it to grasp that multitudinous past of innumerable successions of human beings . . . About her there is the elusive quality of a legend of long ago; some enchantment seems to have held her mind. She is a myth and an idea, a dream and a vision, and yet very real and present and pervasive.[51]

This is evidently a gendered language of mystique. Nehru imbues India with a veiled, feminine metaphor which transmogrifies into the image of an enchanting, modern democracy. Philosophically, the most interesting aspect of the passage is that Nehru ends his intellectual quest for the idea of India with a question. He returns to the question he asks at the beginning, realizing that the meaning of a place and its history can't be appropriated by objective knowledge. The admission of this impossibility involves a deep irony (and ironic failure) which, to Nehru's credit, he acknowledges. Nehru's 'presumptuous' attempt to grasp India does not end on a futile note. His failure is not a philosophical one. Nehru ends with a question, which is always an invitation to think further. Thinking is more fundamental than knowledge. The realization that India cannot be discovered registers the limits of nationalist historiography. Nehru knew that human reality does not correspond to rationalist certainties. Octavio Paz reiterates the depth of this understanding:

> Nehru's life was a series of affirmations but his thought a renewed question about himself and India. He was faithful to his contradictions and for this very reason he neither killed others nor mutilated himself. We all know in order to suppress our contradictors we must begin to suppress the internal contradictor we carry within.[52]

Partha Chatterjee's dismissive tone of observation that *The Discovery* is a book of 'rambling, bristling with the most obvious contradictions',[53] is bad judgement on two counts.

Firstly, what Chatterjee calls 'rambling' can be a genuine predicament for a writer who does not follow a strictly ideological method of enquiry. There is a suggestive coherence in Nehru's 'rambling', if we do not impose a disciplinary and ideological protocol on the writing. In *The Discovery*, Nehru is not just writing history but also providing a modern ethic of life and social relations. He analyses the past from a modernist perspective. He weighs the present vis-à-vis certain desirable tendencies that were evident to him in the past. This double direction of critique extends the scope of historical discourse.

Secondly, Nehru's 'obvious' contradictions are enlightening. The contradictions are proof of the limits to objectivist knowledge. Contradictions illuminate the limits of modern, progressive and scientific thought. One cannot rationally explain the world. Any defeat in the Hegelian sense—when objective knowledge faces its limits—is a Nietzschean triumph.

The idea of India overwhelms Nehru's intentionality. It tells Nehru that an idea is always in excess of what you demand from it. The desire to know everything can end in nothing. It can leave you with empty hands. Nehru realized that India is not an object of total possession (or comprehension). The desired object (of thought, power) eludes the madness for possession. Reason is prone to this madness. There are limits to objectivity that objectivity does well to realize.

Nehru ends *The Discovery* on that Socratic note of realization. He discovers that like identity, culture and history, India is not *just one thing*.

Coda

I am tempted to end the book on this Socratic note. We, however, don't live in Socratic times. Recently, a north-Indian cab driver in Kolkata said in Hindi, before dropping me off at the weary, red-bricked Howrah Railway Station as the sun set behind the Hooghly: 'An Indian politician need not be educated. He can well be a thumb-impression guy.' Was he endorsing, or decrying, the lack of literacy in a political leader? Did he mean politics has nothing to do with education?

His point of view got clearer when he said: 'Nothing is fair and just in India. Educated bureaucrats bend their knees before unlettered politicians.'

The cab driver was being ironic. He was unhappy with illiterate leaders controlling educated but corrupt bureaucrats. The current trend of populism didn't impress him. Lack of literacy alone, however, does not determine an ineffective and unenlightening political leader and regime. The competition for power in democracies induces chronic instrumentality. People lower their ethical standards and use any means to gain power.

The problem becomes more acute in theocratic, communist and fascist regimes. Thought control is crucial to these forms of government. Ideas considered deviant or challenging the ideological order of God, Party, or Nation, is considered anathema and ruthlessly suppressed. Thinking, and the free expression of language, has faced persecution from such forms of power throughout history. In the light of this danger, Nehru's warning is pertinent to this moment of our political history:

> [We] need not go to the past to find instances of the manipulation of history to suit particular ends and support one's own fancies and prejudices. The present is full of this, and if the present, which we have ourselves seen and experienced, can be so distorted, what of the past?[54]

In Nehru's time, manipulative tendencies came chiefly from colonial historians. Nationalist historians, on the other hand, despite their anti-colonial consciousness, suffered a modernist ambivalence: they critiqued the colonial project, but accepted Western ideas as a superior tool of political and social knowledge. This uncritical acceptance produced a uniform ideological lens through which Indian history came to be understood. Within the rationalist mode of analysis, the important *cultural* difference between Europe's medieval age and India's precolonial past became irrelevant. Material conditions got sole prominence. Economic life under feudalism became the focal point of analyses. This approach made us sensitive to the question of labour and power relations in society. India's rich cultural history, the Indo-Islamic encounter, in particular, deserves more intellectual recognition. The Hindu right, in turn, reduced the idea of history to communal sentiment, denied the contribution of other religious identities, and made Hindus the sole claimant of India's cultural heritage. It borrowed the crudest ideas from modern Europe: race and territoriality.[55]

There is a move to redefine Indian history today. New manipulations are underway to undermine the Nehruvian spirit of democracy that has been in crisis since 1984. The clock is being turned back more decisively. History's gaze upon us—to quote W.B. Yeats—is 'blank and pitiless as the sun'.[56]

Acknowledgements

The course on Indian nationalism by Rajeev Bhargava in the summer of 1997 in JNU finally made me read Nehru's *The Discovery of India*. I was intrigued and impressed enough to study Nehru's thoughts for my MPhil dissertation, and later, contrast Nehru with Gandhi for my PhD thesis.

Ramesh acknowledged my interest in Nehru during the years I was writing my MPhil thesis and offered his insights on our many walks in JNU. While having Irani chai together at Sodabottleopenerwala in Khan Market in October 2021, Abir reminded me that I must address Nehru's troubled relationship with Kashmir. Sharmadip's suggestion that I read Nietzsche's views on history was timely and accurate. My conversations over the years with Bidhan and Mohinder on India's political history have been enriching. The best intellectual friendships are fostered by the delight of provocation. The agreements, expressed or unexpressed, remain partial.

I am indebted to my endorsers—Talal Asad, Gopal Guru, Sudipta Kaviraj and Rajeev Bhargava—for reading the manuscript and offering their kind remarks in the middle of other responsibilities. Their attention is a privilege. I am moved by Talal's warm gesture of finding time to read and encourage my work, despite the daily agony of his wife's passing away, and his health constraints.

Richa's insistence made me realize this was the most appropriate time to write on Nehru. The editors at Penguin were warmly professional: Premanka's compliment for the manuscript gave me confidence. Meru was most cordial about the date of publication. Aparna's thoughtful and precise suggestions improved the structure and content of the book. Binita's sensitive editing kept it closest to perfect. Aayushi has proofread with care. I am grateful.

Notes

Introduction: The Man Who Discovered India

1   What Columbus accidentally discovered in 1492 was a sea route across
    the Pacific. The discovery violently interrupted the life of other peoples,
    America's natives, as Columbus did not hesitate to indulge in trans-
    Atlantic slave trade and the genocide of Hispaniola's natives. The Cape
    of Good Hope was good for da Gama, who followed the clues left by
    Bartolomeu Dias ten years earlier and found a trade route to India in
    1497, bypassing the Muslim territories of the Mediterranean Sea and
    the Arabian Peninsula. This eventually led to British colonialism.

2   Hall, Stuart, 'The West and the Rest', in *Modernity: An Introduction
    to Modern Societies*, edited by Stuart Hall, David Held, Don Huburt
    and Kenneth Thompson, Blackwell, Oxford, 1996, page 186.

3   Anderson, Perry, *Indian Ideology* (Expanded Edition), Verso, New
    York, 2021, Kindle edition.

4   Thapar, Romila, 'India's Past and Present: How History
    Informs Contemporary Narrative", in conversation with David
    M. Malone, 2010, available at https://www.youtube.com/
    watch?v=J8HhLJzpx3Y&t=3243s. [Also mentioned in Thapar,
    Romila, 'Ashoka: A Retrospective', *Economic and Political Weekly*,
    Vol. 44, No. 45 (7–13 November 2009), page 35.]

5   Ibid.

6   Thapar, Romila, *The Penguin History of Early India: From The Origins to AD 1300*, Penguin Books, New Delhi, 2002, page 4.

7   Ibid.

8   Ibid., page 5.

9   Hegel, Georg Wilhelm Friedrich, *Philosophy of Right*, translated by S.W. Dyde, Cosmo Classics, New York, 2008, page 201.

10   Anderson, Perry, *Indian Ideology* (Expanded Edition), Verso, NY, 2021, Kindle edition.

11   Ibid.

12   Nandy, Ashis, '"Cultural Frames for Social Intervention": A Personal Credo', *Indian Philosophical Quarterly*, Vol. 11, No. 4, October 1984, page 420.

13   Anderson, Perry, *Indian Ideology* (Expanded Edition), Verso, NY, 2021, Kindle edition.

14   Ibid.

15   Nag, Sajal, 'Nehru and the Nagas: Minority Nationalism and the Post-Colonial State', *Economic and Political Weekly*, Vol. 44, No. 49 (5–11 December 2009), page 52. (My emphasis.)

16   Ibid., page 50.

17   Anderson, Perry, *Indian Ideology* (Expanded Edition), Verso, NY, 2021, Kindle edition.

18   Ibid.

19   Godse, Nathuram, *Why I Killed Gandhi*, Srishti Publishers & Distributors, New Delhi, 2020, Kindle edition.

20   Ibid.

21   Gandhi's sources of ahimsa were the Jain and Christian (*Sermon on the Mount*) traditions. Ambedkar drew his idea of ahimsa from his reading of the Buddha. Gandhi's idea of nonviolence was an individual ethic, whereas Ambedkar saw nonviolence in a more social sense, against the violence of caste and discrimination.

22   Anderson, Perry, *Indian Ideology* (Expanded Edition), Verso, NY, 2021, Kindle edition.

23   Guha, Ramachandra, *India after Gandhi: The History of the World's Largest Democracy*, Picador, London, 2007, page 60.

24   Ibid., page 61.

25   Ibid.

26 Ibid., page 70.
27 Ibid., pages 71–72.
28 Ibid., pages 72–73.
29 Ibid., page 76.
30 Ibid., page 78.
31 Ibid., page 244.
32 Ibid.
33 Ibid., page 246.
34 Ibid., page 247.
35 Ibid.
36 Ibid., page 248.
37 Ibid., page 249.
38 Ibid., page 250.
39 Ibid., page 251.
40 Ibid., pages 253–254.
41 Ibid., page 255.
42 Ibid.
43 Ibid.
44 Ibid., page 256.
45 Ibid.
46 Crocker, Walter, *Nehru: A Contemporary Estimate*, Vintage, Penguin Random House, New Delhi, 2008, page 140.
47 Derrida, Jacques, *The Politics of Friendship*, translated by George Collins, Verso, London/U.K., 1997, page 88.
48 Crocker, *Nehru: A Contemporary Estimate*, page 183.
49 Montaigne described friendship as 'general and universal warmth, moderate and even . . . with nothing bitter and stinging about it' [De Montaigne, Michel, *The Complete Essays of Montaigne*, translated by Donald M. Frame, Stanford University Press, California, 1958, page 137].
50 Paz, Octavio, 'Nehru: Man of Two Cultures and One World', in International Round Table on Jawaharlal Nehru, New Delhi, 1966, *Nehru and the Modern World* (New Delhi: Indian National Commission for Co-operation with UNESCO, 1967), page 15, https://archive.org/details/in.ernet.dli.2015.159218/page/n15/mode/2up?q=octavio+paz+nehru&view=theater (accessed on 19 February 2022).

51   Malraux, André, *Anti-Memoirs*, translated by Terance Kilmartin, Holt, Rinehart and Winston, New York, 1968, page 145.

52   Paz, Octavio, 'Nehru: Man of Two Cultures and One World', in International Round Table on Jawaharlal Nehru, New Delhi, 1966, *Nehru and the Modern World* (New Delhi: Indian National Commission for Co-operation with UNESCO, 1967), page 15.

53   Nehru, Jawaharlal, *The Discovery of India*, Oxford University Press, New Delhi, 1964, page 57.

54   Paz, 'Nehru: Man of Two Cultures and One World', page 15.

55   Mao Tse-tung develops the double-edged idea of 'antagonistic contradiction' from Lenin, where on the one hand the contradiction between labour and capital, countryside and town, are seen as antagonistic, but on the other, the class struggle spearheaded by the Communist Party shall also heighten, or intensify, these antagonisms. See https://www.marxists.org/reference/archive/mao/selected-works/volume-1/mswv1_17.htm#bm25.

56   Paz, 'Nehru: Man of Two Cultures and One World', page 14.

57   Ambedkar, Dr B.R., 'The Annihilation of Caste', in *Dr. Babasaheb Ambedkar Writings and Speeches*, Vol. 1. Education Department, Government of Maharashtra, Bombay, 14 April 1979, page 59.

58   Chisick, Harvey, 'Ethics and History in Voltaire's Attitudes toward the Jews', *Eighteenth-Century Studies*, Vol. 35, No. 4 (Summer, 2002), The Johns Hopkins University Press, page 589.

59   Ibid., page 590.

60   See Gunn, T. Jeremy, 'Do Human Rights Have a Secular, Individualistic and Anti-Islamic Bias?', *Daedalus*, Vol. 149, No. 3 (2020), pages 148–169.

61   Nehru, *The Discovery of India*, page 519.

62   Ibid.

63   Ibid.

64   Ibid.

65   Nietzsche, Fredrich, *The Use and Abuse of History*, page 44.

66   Ibid.

67   The individual without a community is not only nothing, but absurd. For Samuel Beckett, Albert Camus and Jean-Paul Sartre, like many other writers of twentieth-century Europe, the experience of absurdity, the despairing confession that life is meaningless and

absurd and useless, were warnings of what the individual faces in a modern culture that is celebrated in the name of individualism. *The absurdity of modernity is the absurdity of the individual.* [In Albert Camus's *The Myth of Sisyphus* and *The Rebel*, absurdity comes from a lack of 'experience' (https://plato.stanford.edu/entries/camus/). I would add, cultural experience. In Jean-Paul Sartre's *Nausea* (1938), Antoine Roquentin discovers absurdity like a plague of modern life. The futility of experience, of existence, is what reason failed to deliver for lack of culture. In Samuel Beckett's play *Waiting for Godot* (1952), the absurd is explained through the act of waiting *for no one*. In Abbas Kiarostami's *Taste of Cherry* (1997), Mr Badii's difficulties in looking for a man to bury him evokes the absurd. Emily Durkheim's term 'anomie' relates to the lack of 'common meanings' (https://www.britannica.com/topic/anomie).]

68 See https://thewire.in/politics/why-hindutva-is-a-racist-supremacism-not-a-communalism-or-majoritarianism.

69 I would like to steer clear of the minor being read in terms of anything 'collective' that connects to a revolutionary idea or theory, except perhaps as what Deleuze and Guattari calls 'revolutionary force' (*Kafka: Toward a Minor Literature*, translated by Dana Polan, University of Minnesota Press, Minneapolis, page 19).

70 Deleuze, Gilles, Guatarri, Félix, *Kafka: Toward a Minor Literature*, translated by Dana Polan, University of Minnesota Press, Minneapolis, page 19.

Chapter 1: Colonialism and 'the Garb of Modernity'

1 'Does the God of Learning Drink Milk?', by The Associated Press, *New York Times*, 22 September 1995, https://www.nytimes.com/1995/09/22/world/does-the-god-of-learning-drink-milk.html (accessed on 19 February 2022).

2 Burns, John F., 'India's "Guru Busters" Debunk All That's Mystical', *New York Times*, 10 October 1995.

3 Bocock, Robert, 'The Cultural Formations of Modern Society', in *Modernity: An Introduction to Modern Societies*, edited by Stuart Hall, David Held, Don Hubert and Kenneth Thompson, Blackwell, Oxford, 1996, page 175.

4   Ibid.

5   Weber, Max, *The Protestant Ethic and the Spirit of Capitalism*, translated by Talcott Parsons, Routledge Classics, New York, 2001, page 72.

6   Ibid., page 96.

7   H.F. describes how a terror-ridden people facing the avalanche of the plague were exploited by 'Fortune Tellers, Cunning Men and Astrologers, to know their Fortune, or as 'tis vulgarly express'd, to have their Fortunes told them . . . and this Folly, presently made the Town swarm with a wicked Generation of Pretenders to Magic, to the *Black Art, as they call'd it*'. Despite being a religious man, H.F. calls these practices 'blind, absurd and ridiculous Stuff' and 'Oracles of the Devil' [Defoe, Daniel, *A Journal of the Plague Year*, Modern Library, New York, 2001, page 27].

8   Bocock, 'The Cultural Formations of Modern Society', page 175.

9   Surrealism is originally associated with Guillaume Apollinaire (who coined the term in 1917) and André Breton, who wrote *The Surrealist Manifesto* in 1924.

10   Freud, Sigmund, *The Uncanny*, edited by David Mclintock, Penguin Books, London, 2003, page 148.

11   Griffin, Roger, 'Series Editor's Preface', in John Bramble, *Modernism and the Occult*, Basingstoke: Palgrave Macmillan, 2015, page xii.

12   André Breton wrote: 'Under the pretense of civilization and progress, we have managed to banish from the mind everything that may rightly or wrongly be termed superstition or fancy; forbidden is any kind of search for the truth which is not in conformance with accepted practices' [André Breton, *First Manifesto of Surrealism in Art in Theory 1900– 1990: An Anthology of Changing Ideas*, edited by Charles Harrison and Paul Wood, Blackwell Publishers, Oxford, 1992, page 87].

        In the Latin-American hemisphere, literature in the 1920s is associated with the term 'magic realism' after the publication of works by María Luisa Bombal, Gabriel García Márquez, Isabel Allende and Jorge Luis Borges and others. Magic realism is, however, a popular misrepresentation. It is a binary between magic and realism, retained to serve the West's self-conscious distinction: magic deemed to be medieval, and realism deemed to be modern. The proper term for that literature was given by the Cuban novelist Alejo Carpentier, 'lo real marvilloso' (marvellously real, or marvellous real), where 'marvellous' does not suggest something other than real, but something within the ordinary aspects of real life. Carpentier contrasted it with surrealism: 'To begin with, the phenomenon of the marvelous presupposes faith. Those who do not believe in saints cannot cure themselves with the miracles of saints . . . Therefore it seems the marvelous invoked in disbelief—the case of the Surrealists for so many years—was never anything more than a literary ruse' [Carpentier, Alejo, 'On the Marvelous Real in America', in *Magical Realism: Theory History, Community*, edited by Lois Parkinson Zamora and Wendy B. Faris, Duke University Press, Durham & London, 1995, page 86].

13   Nehru, Jawaharlal, *The Discovery of India*, Oxford University Press, New Delhi, 1994, page 25.

14   Ibid., page 28.

15   Ibid., page 26.

16   Ibid., page 513.

17   Ibid., page 511.

18   Ibid., pages 511–12.

19   Ibid., page 519.

20   Ibid., pages 519–20.

21   Ibid., page 518.

22   'ISRO Scientists Superstitious, Follow Rahu Kaalam, Unlucky 13 before Rocket Launch: Former Official', *India Today*, 21 July 2019, https://www.indiatoday.in/science/chandrayaan-2-mission/story/isro-scientists-superstitious-follow-rahu-kaalam-unlucky-13-before-rocket-launch-former-official-1571882-2019-07-21 (accessed on 19 February 2022).

23   Dutt, Anonna, '"15 Mins of Terror", Says ISRO Chief on Chandrayaan 2 Moon Landing', *Hindustan Times*, 26 June 2020, https://www.hindustantimes.com/india-news/chandrayaan-2-moon-landing-15-minutes-of-terror-await/story-q1dkjNSdyOrU8SyUhosGeI.html (accessed on 19 February 2022).

24   Bhattacharjee, Manash Firaq, 'The Closed Doors of Caste in India', *The Wire*, 5 June 2019, https://thewire.in/caste/payal-tadvi-discrimination-suicide (accessed on 19 February 2022).

25   Sukanya, Santha, 'Payal Tadvi Case: Chargesheet Reveals Months of Humiliation, Discrimination', *The Wire*, 25 July 2019, https://

thewire.in/rights/dr-payal-tadvi-suicide-chargesheet (accessed on 19 February 2022).

26   Nehru, *The Discovery of India*, page 121.

27   Ibid., page 84.

28   Ibid., page 226.

29   Ibid., page 257.

30   Ibid., page 85.

31   Kosambi, D.D. *Combined Methods in Indology and Other Writings*, Oxford University Press, New Delhi, 2002, page 59.

32   Chakrabarty, Dipesh, *Habitations of Modernity*, The University of Chicago Press, Chicago, 2002, page 27.

33   Ibid., pages 27–28.

34   Nehru, *The Discovery of India*, page 291.

35   Ibid. (My emphasis.)

36   Gilmour, David, *The British in India: A Social History of the Raj*, Picador, New York, 2019, page 525.

37   Ibid.

38   'Minute by the Hon'ble T. B. Macaulay, dated the 2nd February 1835', http://www.columbia.edu/itc/mealac/pritchett/00generallinks/macaulay/txt_minute_education_1835.html (accessed on 19 February 2022).

39   I won't say 'transformed' as transformation involves agency and a sense of becoming.

40   Nehru, *The Discovery of India*, page 564.

41   Kaviraj, Sudipta, *The Enchantment of Democracy and India Politics and Ideas*, Permanent Black, New Delhi, 2018, Kindle edition.

42   Bhabha, Homi K., *The Location of Culture*, Routledge Classics, New York, 1994, page 85.

43   Ibid.

44   Chatterjee, Partha, *The Nation and Its Fragments: Colonial and Postcolonial Histories*, Princeton University Press, Princeton, New Jersey, 1993, page 6.

45   Ibid.

46   Ibid.

47   Nietzsche, Fredrich, *The Use and Abuse of History*, translated by Adrian Collins, Bobbs-Merrill Company: Liberal Arts Press, New York, 1957 (second revised edition), page 28.

48   Ibid., page 24.

49   Tejani, Shabnum, *Indian Secularism: A Social and Intellectual History, 1890–1950*, Permanent Black, Delhi, 2007.

50   Ibid., page 48.

51   Ibid., page 54.

52   Ibid., page 35.

53   Ibid.

54   Rimbaud, Arthur, *Collected Poems*, translated by Martin Sorell, Oxford University Press, New York, 2001, page 253.

There is an illustration of Rimbaud's statement by Dipesh Chakrabarty in an Indian context. He recounts the amusing story told by the Bengali writer Nirad C. Chaudhuri, in his autobiographical sequel *Thy Hand, Great Anarch!* about his wedding night. To avert the moment of awkwardness with a stranger in a traditional marriage, Chaudhuri takes recourse to his taste in Western culture. He asks his wife if she has heard of Beethoven. When she replies in the affirmative, he asks her like a circumspect Englishman to spell his name. Chakrabarty writes: 'The desire to be "modern" screams out of every sentence.' The episode showcases the obsession of the Indian elite to mimic the colonial master. [Chakrabarty, Dipesh, *Representations*, No. 37, Special Issue: Imperial Fantasies and Postcolonial Histories (Winter, 1992), page 10. Published by University of California Press.]

55   Kundera, Milan, *Immortality*, translated by Peter Kussi, Harper Perennial Classics, New York, 1999, page 138.

56   Tagore, Rabindranath, *Nationalism*, Penguin Random House, New Delhi, 2009, page 41.

57   Ibid., page 39.

58   Ibid., page 86.

59   Kaviraj, Sudipta, 'Modernity and Politics in India', *Daedalus*, Vol. 129, No. 1, Multiple Modernities (Winter, 2000), page 141.

60   Ibid., page 153.

61   Modernity imbued with the rational and secular principles of the Enlightenment also created an ethically fraught subject in the West as well. It made Western intellectuals probe deep into the problems of the modern subject. One argument that emerges from a vast discussion on the subject by Charles Taylor in his famous work *Sources of the Self: The Making of the Modern Identity* is the problem of the absence

of an overarching, or constitutive idea of the good. Taylor looks for the elusive principle of the good in modernity by critically evaluating Utilitarianism, Naturalism, Kant and the Romantics.

Scottish philosopher Alastair MacIntyre raised two issues with Taylor's thesis that concerns our discussion on modernity. The first problem he locates in Taylor's question, 'What better measure of reality do we have in human affairs, than those terms which on critical reflection and after correction of the errors we can detect make the best sense of our lives?' [188] Macintyre finds this enabling simply 'too many rival ways' [188] to assess what is right for us. Criticality and corrective forms in thinking leaves the problem to be sorted by self-reflective rationality.

It is the abiding predicament of normative philosophers like Taylor and Macintyre that they look for certainties on the question of the good in reason. The ethical dilemma caused by reason here is to precisely be unable to offer judgement on something that the self must consider beyond itself. To make the self the source of the idea of the good is to reduce the problem of ethics to individuality.

Macintyre points out his other problem that Taylor's idea of choosing between more than one goods is ultimately down to 'personal preferences'. Call it preference or choice, it is the same thing. It is luxurious to place the question of choice to personal preference, which is a kind of objective desire. It is not even pure desire, but desire controlled by rational consideration. The positive content of ethics is risk, and it is the risking of rational certainty. But it is not simply the method of trial and error where certainty is an objective goal towards what is correct. In ethics, the self is on trial to overcome the hurdles of reason. In ethics, *reason is the error*. To seek, to reach the place where meeting the other is possible, is what concerns ethics. It is a sensuous and spontaneous consideration. Here, judgement is intuitive, thought is risk prone. In his critique of Taylor, Macintyre is himself caught in the question of 'what makes a choice between them rational?' [188]. Choosing rationally is to calculate. Risk is incalculable. The whole point of ethics is to imagine *being chosen* [see MacIntyre, Alastair, 'Critical Remarks on *The Sources of the Self* by Charles Taylor', *Philosophy and Phenomenological Research*, Vol. 54, No. 1, March 1994, pages 187–190].

62   Asad, Talal, 'Modern Power and the Reconfiguration of Religious Traditions', interview with Saba Mahmood, *SEHR*, Vol. 5, Issue 1: Contested Polities, 27 February 1996.

63   Schmitt, Carl, *Political Theology: Four Chapters on the Concept of Sovereignty*, translated by George Schwab, MIT Press, Cambridge, Massachusetts, 1985, page 36.

64   Walter Benjamin writes: 'The Messiah comes not only as the redeemer, he comes as the subduer of Antichrist. Only that historian will have the gift of fanning the spark of hope in the past who is firmly convinced that even the dead will not be safe from the enemy if he wins' [Benjamin, Walter, *Illuminations*, edited by Hannah Arendt, Schocken Books (Random House Inc.), New York, 1969, page 255]. Benjamin evokes a complex figure of the desirable historian, conceived as someone appearing in the shadow of the Messiah. That historian understands the spirit of the past as not contained, or containable, within the conformist norms of tradition, and speaks for a past that can be freed from the clutches of the conformists. Like the Messiah, Benjamin's desirable historian gifts us a present that not only frees us from the past, but frees the past from itself.

65   Emanuel Levinas, in his seminal work *Totality and Infinity*, understands the meaning of being I, as a 'metaphysical desire [that] tends toward something else entirely, towards the absolutely other' [Emanuel Levinas, *Totality and Infinity: An Essay on Exteriority*, Martinus Nijhoff Publishers, The Hague, 1979, page 33]. The desire of the I is understood by Levinas as something other than the idea of the I. This desire creates alterity. An idea of the I leads you back to the I. But desire leads you *away from* the I. This desire introduces 'the alterity of the Other and of the Most-High' [Ibid., page 34]. The Other breaks through the limits of rationalist knowledge, and haunts us with a desire that is metaphysical in nature. We can also understand desire here as seeking.

66   Nehru, *The Discovery of India*, page 53.

67   Ibid., page 557.

68   The answer to this question is summed up between two famous statements by the Russian writer Fyodor Dostoevsky. In a well-known lecture given in 1946, Jean-Paul Sartre reminded his readers of what Dostoevsky wrote in *The Brothers Karamazov*: 'If God did not exist,

everything would be permitted.' Sartre's philosophical optimism for human freedom, arises from this statement. The absence of god, or a divine power, suggests that there is no obligation to be good. In philosophical terms, it means there is no *a priori* idea of human good, human essence, or human nature, to fall back on. Since there is no 'infinite and perfect' divinity, nothing pre-given determines our existence and our actions. We are purely free. As Sartre puts it, we are free 'without excuse'. Freedom, in Sartre's view, alone determines the good. Freedom alone is human essence, and human nature [Quotations from Jean-Paul Sartre 1946 (lecture), 'Existentialism Is a Humanism', translated by Philip Mairet, 2005, https://www. marxists.org/reference/archive/sartre/works/exist/sartre.htm (accessed on 19 February 2022)].

But (how) can freedom determine human goodness? This question leads us to the next famous sentence by Alyosha Karamazov in Dostoevsky's *The Brothers Karamazov*, a favourite reference of the French ethical thinker Emanuel Levinas: 'Each of us is guilty before everyone for everyone, and I more than the others' [Levinas, Emanuel, *Otherwise Than Being: Or Beyond Essence*, translated by Alphonso Lingis, Duquesne University Press, Pittsburg, Pennsylvania, 1981, page 146]. In other translations of this quote, the word 'responsibility' is used for 'guilty'. The ethical point Levinas makes from this sentence is that there is an asymmetry of responsibility that involves one's relationship with the other, and the world of others. Before calling the world into question, one calls oneself into question. This ethical responsibility is not strictly circumstantial, or historical (or political in the narrow sense), but a consideration that comes *prior to* everything. Sartre uses a somewhat similar argument in his lecture mentioned earlier, and goes on to define an ethic of freedom based on our absolute responsibility towards fellow human beings. This deep sense of responsibility can be extended towards everything else, including our beliefs, and desires.

69   Paz, Octavio, 'Nehru: Man of Two Cultures and One World', in International Round Table on Jawaharlal Nehru, New Delhi, 1966, *Nehru and the Modern World*, New Delhi: Indian National Commission for Co-operation with UNESCO, 1967, page 16.

70   Ibid.

71   Nehru, *An Autobiography*, Oxford University Press, New Delhi, 1980, page 19.

72   Ibid.

73   Ibid., page 20.

74   Paz, 'Nehru: Man of Two Cultures and One World', page 16.

75   Nehru, *An Autobiography*, page 1.

76   Ibid., page 3.

77   Ibid., page 8.

78   Ibid., page 13.

79   Ibid., page 596.

80   Rimbaud, Arthur, *Collected Poems*, translated by Martin Sorell, Oxford University Press, New York, 2001, page 253.

81   Crocker, Walter, *Nehru: A Contemporary's Estimate*, Vintage, Delhi, 2008, page 133.

82   Nehru, *The Discovery of India*, page 49.

83   Paz, Octavio, *Alternating Current*, Arcade Publishing, New York, 1990, page 198.

84   Ibid., page 50.

85   V.D. Savarkar raised the question, 'Who is a Hindu?' The question is tackled in genealogical terms, by going back to the concept of the 'Aryans', a sacred sense of territoriality and a historical sense of identity where the Hindu is one who is not the 'others' he confronts—namely Muslims, Christians, who are considered outsiders. The question of good or bad, more or less, follows from there. The purer the identity, the better it is [*Hindutva: Who is a Hindu?*, Veer Savarkar Prakashan, Savarkar Sadan, Bombay, 1969].

86   https://plato.stanford.edu/entries/kant-transcendental-idealism/.

87   Nehru, *The Discovery of India*, page 49.

88   Tagore, Rabindranath, *Letters from Russia*, translated by Sasadhar Sinha, Vishva-Bharati, Calcutta, 1960, page 64.

Chapter 2: The Citizen and the 'Secular State Business'

1   Jayal, Niraja Gopal, 'Faith-Based Citizenship: The Dangerous Path India is Choosing', *The India Forum*, Issue: 1 November 2019, https://www.theindiaforum.in/article/faith-criterion-citizenship (accessed on 19 February 2022).

2   Ibid.

3   Ibid.

4   Roy, Anupama, *Mapping Citizenship in India*, Oxford University Press, New Delhi 2010, Kindle edition.

5   Ibid.

6   Ibid.

7   Jayal, 'Faith-Based Citizenship'.

8   See https://ruralindiaonline.org/library/resource/articles-5-11-part-ii-in-the-constituent-assembly-of-india-debates-proceedings-volume-ix---august-10-11-and-12-1949/ (accessed on 19 February 2022).

9   Ibid.

10   Ibid.

11   Ibid.

12   Ibid.

13   Ibid.

14   Ibid.

15   Ibid.

16   Ibid.

17   Ibid.

18   Ibid.

19   Ibid.

20   Ibid.

21   Ibid.

22   Ibid.

23   Ibid.

24   Ibid.

25   Ibid.

26   Ibid.

27   Ibid.

28   See http://164.100.47.194/loksabha/writereaddata/cadebatefiles/C04111948.html (accessed on 19 February 2022).

29   See http://164.100.47.194/Loksabha/Debates/cadebatefiles/C05111948.html (accessed on 19 February 2022).

30   See https://ruralindiaonline.org/library/resource/articles-5-11-part-ii-in-the-constituent-assembly-of-india-debates-proceedings-volume-ix---august-10-11-and-12-1949/ (accessed on 19 February 2022).

31   Rushdie, Salman, *Shame*, Vintage, London, 1995, page 87.

32   See https://indiankanoon.org/doc/1993069/.

33   Ibid.

34   Ibid.

35   Ibid. (My emphasis.)

36   Ibid.

37   Kolsky, Elizabeth, 'The Colonial Rule of Law and the Legal Regime of Exception: Frontier "Fanaticism" and State Violence in British India', *The American Historical Review*, October 2015, page 1223.

38   Singh, Tripurdaman, Hussain, Adeel, *Nehru: The Debates that Defined India*, Fourth Estate, New Delhi, 2021, Kindle edition.

39   Agamben expands on the term he borrows from Walter Benjamin (as described in different translations as "state of emergency" and "state of exception" from "On the Concept of History"/"Thesis on the Philosophy of History") and Carl Schmitt. The state of exception includes the "question of borders" [Agamben, Giorgio, *State of Exception*, (trans.) Kevin Attell, The University of Chicago Press, Chicago and London, 2005, page 1.]

40   See https://indiankanoon.org/doc/215406/ (accessed on 19 February 2022).

41   Ibid.

42   Ibid.

43   Chawla, Abhay, 'How Meos Shape Their Identity', *Economic and Political Weekly*, Vol. 51, No. 10, 5 March 2016.

44   'Constituent Assembly Debates on 12 August, 1949, Part I', indiankanoon.org/doc/215406/.

45   Ibid.

46   Ibid.

47   Ibid.

48   See Bhattacharjee, Manash Firaq, 'We Foreigners: What It Means to Be Bengali in India's Assam', *Aljazeera*, 26 February 2020, https://www.aljazeera.com/features/2020/2/26/we-foreigners-what-it-means-to-be-bengali-in-indias-assam (accessed on 19 February 2022).

49   Siddique, Nazimuddin, 'A Response to Hiren Gohain: The NRC Is a Product of Xenophobia in Assam', *Economic and Political Weekly*, Vol. 55, Issue No. 14 (4 April 2020), https://www.epw.in/engage/article/response-hiren-gohain-nrc-product-xenophobia-assam (accessed on 19 February 2022).

50   See Bhargava, Rajeev, 'Should Europe Learn from Indian Secularism?',
      Seminar, 2011, https://www.india-seminar.com/2011/621/621_
      rajeev_bhargava.htm (accessed on 19 February 2022).

51   Katzenstein, Mary F., 'Origins of Nativism: The Emergence of Shiv
      Sena in Bombay', *Asian Survey*, Vol. 13, No. 4 (April 1973), pages
      386–399.

52   See Bhargava, Rajeev, 'Should Europe Learn from Indian Secularism?',
      Seminar, 2011, https://www.india-seminar.com/2011/621/621_
      rajeev_bhargava.htm.

53   See Basu, Upmanyu, 'The Forgotten Exodus—Conflict of Kashmir
      Valley and Kashmiri Pandits', *The Geopolitics*, 11 October 2020,
      https://thegeopolitics.com/the-forgotten-exodus-conflict-of-kashmir-
      valley-and-kashmiri-pandits/ (accessed on 19 February 2022).

54   See Fareed, Rifat, 'The Forgotten Massacre that Ignited the Kashmir
      Dispute', *Aljazeera*, 6 November 2017, https://www.aljazeera.com/
      news/2017/11/6/the-forgotten-massacre-that-ignited-the-kashmir-
      dispute (accessed on 19 February 2022).

55   See 'Mass Murder in Sunderban: Marichjhanpi', Activist Canvas
      (blog), https://canvaspix.wordpress.com/2011/05/24/marichjhanpi/
      (accessed on 19 February 2022).

56   Kimura, Makiko, *The Nellie Massacre of 1983*: *Agency of Rioters*, Sage
      Publications, New Delhi, 2013, page 1.

57   See Bhattacharjee, Manash Firaq, 'And Quiet Flows the Kopili:
      Violence and Citizenship in Assam, as Experienced by Its Forgotten',
      Guernica, 24 September 2015, https://www.guernicamag.com/
      manash-bhattacharjee-and-quiet-flows-the-kopili/ (accessed on 19
      February 2022).

58   Noorani, A.G., *The Destruction of Hyderabad*, Tulika Books, New
      Delhi, 2013, page 2.

59   Ibid., page 195.

60   Ibid.

61   Ibid.

62   Nehru, Jawaharlal, *Letters for a Nation: From Jawaharlal Nehru to
      His Chief Ministers 1947–1963*, edited by Madhav Khosla, Penguin
      India, New Delhi, 2014, page 202.

63   Ibid.

64   Ibid., page 203.

65   Ibid., page 214.
66   In a letter dated, 16 April 1948, Nehru wrote to his Defence Minister, Baldev Singh:

    I wish to avoid, as you must also do, any action on our part which might be construed as indicating aggression on Hyderabad State. Nevertheless, we have to be prepared to protect our people . . . The main part of the force . . . is the armoured brigade, and it is necessary that this should be for use if an emergency arises . . . This movement should start soon but it need not be done in a hurried manner as any indication of precipitate action might be misunderstood and might bring about a crisis which the move is intended to avoid. Ibid., page 186.

67   Ibid., page 223.
68   Rimbaud, Arthur, *Collected Poems*, translated by Martin Sorell, Oxford University Press, New York, 2001, page xvii.
69   This radical thought that comes from Rimbaud makes otherness intrinsic to the meaning of identity. It moves away from the understanding of identity in German Idealism where I is posited or situated as I, a matter of unity between subject and object, as idea, with nothing other to it. 'I is I' is a logical formulation, based on reason. In its absolute sense, I is an Absolute Idea for Hegel, a totality that is history. Heidegger understands identity as 'belonging' to Being and is measured in its *difference* from the real, historical world of beings. I is *not* reducible to the Hegelian Absolute, or any totality that is history. Even though Heidegger breaks away from Hegel's formulation of identity, it is still a lonely concept. Heidegger doesn't push the idea of difference to posit, or situate, a subject that is dialogic, an idea of Being that is constituted (and haunted) by what it cannot possess and yet that which exists before him, precisely, the other. In real, historical (and anthropological) terms, identity is marked by what limits it, and what differentiates it from the other. Ethics is a positive recognition of this difference. See Heidegger, Martin, *Identity and Difference*, translated by Joan Stambaugh, Harper & Row, New York, 1969.
70   'My point is, of course I understand what's at stake for the Muslim community. But that's because the basic idea of Indian pluralism is threatened. Broadbase the cause. You can't fight Hindutva communalism by promoting Muslim communalism. Identity

politics will destroy India' [30 December 2019], https://twitter.com/shashitharoor/status/1211647018332016643 (accessed on 19 February 2022).

71   Tejani, Shabnum, *Indian Secularism: A Social and Intellectual History, 1890–1950*, Permanent Black, Delhi, 2007, page 13.

72   Ibid., page 2.

73   Ambedkar, Babasaheb, *Dr. Babasaheb Ambedkar Writings and Speeches Vol. 1*, Education Department, Govt. of Maharashtra, Bombay, 14 April, 1979, page 427.

74   Tejani, Shabnum, *Indian Secularism: A Social and Intellectual History, 1890–1950*, Permanent Black, Delhi, 2007, page 238.

75   Ibid., page 186.

76   Ibid., pages 186–187.

77   Ibid., page 2. Tejani writes: 'Communalism was secularism's opposite . . . seen as the antithesis of Indian nationhood.'

78   Fatemah, Hayaat, 'Slogans Like "La Ilaha IlAllah" Narrow the Scope of Anti-CAA Protests', *Indian Express*, 13 January 2020, https://indianexpress.com/article/opinion/columns/citizenship-amendment-act-caa-protests-muslims-6213298/.

79   Ibid.

80   Tharoor clarified and countered various criticisms against his series of tweets (quoted earlier) in an article soon after. But the arguments in the articles are not better articulated than what he already did in his tweets. See Tharoor, Shashi, 'CAA-NRC Protests & Muslims: Why It Can't Only Be Identity Politics', *The Quint*, 13 January 2020, https://www.thequint.com/voices/opinion/caa-nrc-protests-muslims-identity-politics-shashi-tharoor#read-more (accessed on 19 February 2022).

81   PTI, 'CAA Stir: Inter-Faith Prayer to Uphold Values of Preamble as Shaheen Bagh Protest Nears Month', *The Hindu*, 12 January 2020, https://www.thehindu.com/news/national/other-states/caa-stir-inter-faith-prayer-to-uphold-values-of-preamble-as-shaheen-bagh-protest-nears-month/article30551271.ece (accessed on 19 February 2022).

82   Anand, Javed, 'Muslims Are Protesting Not Because Their Religion Is in Danger, but for the Imperilled Constitution', *Indian Express*, 20 January 2020, https://indianexpress.com/article/opinion/columns/

led-by-the-people-indian-constitution-caa-protests-6225047/ (accessed on 19 February 2022).

83   Nehru, Jawaharlal, *The Discovery of India*, Oxford University Press, New Delhi, 1994, pages 381–382.

84   Ibid., page 382.

85   Ibid., page 383.

86   Ibid.

87   Ibid.

88   Ibid.

89   Appadurai, Arjun, *Fear of Small Numbers: An Essay on the Geography of Anger*, Duke University Press, Durham and London, 2006, page 8.

90   Nehru, *The Discovery of India*, page 383.

91   Ibid., page 384.

92   Tejani, *Indian Secularism*, page 14.

93   Ambedkar, Dr. B.R., *Dr. Babasaheb Ambedkar Writings and Speeches*, Vol. 2, Education Department, Government of Maharashtra, Bombay, 1979, page 261.

94   Hussain, Adeel, and Singh, Tripurdaman, *Nehru: The Debates that Defined India*, Fourth Estate, New Delhi, 2021, Kindle edition.

95   Chatterjee, Partha, 'Ambedkar's Theory of Minority Rights', in *The Radical in Ambedkar: Critical Reflections*, edited by Anand Teltumbde and Suraj Yengde, Penguin India/Allen Lane, New Delhi, 2018, page 113.

96   Ibid., page 127.

97   Ibid.

98   Ibid., page 128.

99   Ibid.

100   Nehru, *The Discovery of India*, page 31.

101   Ibid., page 246. (My emphasis.)

102   Tejani, Shabnum, 'The Necessary Conditions for Democracy: B R Ambedkar on Nationalism, Minorities and Pakistan', *Economic and Political Weekly*, Vol. 48, No. 50 (14 December 2013), page 118.

103   Ibid., page 115.

104   Ibid., page 114. Interestingly, Ambedkar quotes from a pamphlet titled 'The Hindu Nationalist Movement' written by Bhai Parmanand, a Hindu Mahasabha leader: 'In history the Hindus revere the memory

of Prithvi Raj, Partap, Shivaji and, Beragi Bir, who fought for the honour and freedom of this land (against the Muslims), while the Mahomedans look upon the invaders of India, like Muhammad Bin Qasim and rulers like Aurangzeb as their national heroes.' Then he goes on to add in his own words: 'In the religious field, the Hindus draw their inspiration from the Ramayan, the Mahabharat and the Geeta. The Musalmans, on the other hand, derive their inspiration from the Quran and the Hadis.' See Ambedkar, Babasaheb, *Pakistan or the Partition of India, Dr. Babasaheb Ambedkar Writings and Speeches*, Vol. 8, Government of Maharashtra, Bombay, 1990, pages 35–46.

105 Ibid., page 116.
106 Ibid., page 118.
107 Ibid., page 119.
108 Ambedkar, *Pakistan or the Partition of India*, pages 330–331.
109 Nehru, *The Discovery of India*, page 62.
110 Ibid., page 244.
111 Ambedkar, *Pakistan or the Partition of India*, page 33.
112 Ibid., page 36.
113 Ibid, page 335.
114 Ibid.
115 Nehru, Jawaharlal, *Letters for a Nation: From Jawaharlal Nehru to His Chief Ministers 1947–1963*, edited by Madhav Khosla, Penguin India, New Delhi, 2014, page 67.
116 Paz, Octavio, *The Labyrinth of Solitude*, translated by Lysander Kemp, Yara Milos and Rachel Phillips Belash, London, 1985, epigraph.
117 Ibid., page 515.
118 Ibid., page 512.
119 Nehru, Jawaharlal, *An Autobiography*, Oxford University Press, New Delhi, 1980, page 169.
120 Shackle, Christopher 'India xviii. Persian Elements in Indian Languages', *Encyclopedia Iranica*, 15 December 15 2004, https://iranicaonline.org/articles/india-xviii-persian-elements-in-indian-languages (accessed on 19 February 2022).
121 Sandel, Michael, 'The Procedural Republic and the Unencumbered Self', *Political Theory*, Vol. 12, No. 1 (February 1984), pages 81–96.
122 Nehru, *The Discovery of India*, page 31.

123 See Nehru, Jawaharlal, 'The Panorama of India's Past', *Seminar*, 2018, https://www.india-seminar.com/2018/704/704_from_nehru's_ writings.ht (accessed on 19 February 2022).

124 Ibid.

125 Jafferlot, Christopher, *The Hindu Nationalist Movement and Indian Politics: 1925 to the 1990s*, Hurst & Company London, 1996, page 102.

126 This makes the evocation of the term 'collective conscience' in relation to the nation a false phrase and idea.

127 Hussain, Adeel, and Singh, Tripurdaman, *Nehru: The Debates that Defined India*, Fourth Estate, New Delhi, 2021, Kindle edition.

128 Christopher, *The Hindu Nationalist Movement and Indian Politics*, page 102.

129 Bilgrami, Akeel, 'Two Concepts of Secularism', *Economic and Political Weekly*, Vol. 29, No. 28 (9 July 1994), page 1753.

130 Ibid., page 1754.

131 Nehru, *The Discovery of India*, page 392.

132 Ibid.

133 See https://eparlib.nic.in/bitstream/123456789/58338/1/ jcb_1951_constitution_1st_amendment_bill.pdf.

134 Sunil Khilnani understands the 'principle of positive discrimination' as 'compensation for past injuries' that weakened 'universal rights' granted to 'individual rights and equality' [Khilnani, Sunil, *The Idea of India*, Penguin India, New Delhi, 2004, page 36]. This prejudice is shared by many liberals who do not recognize that caste-based structures of power and discrimination are not 'past' but very much alive in the present. The idea of equality is not only based on the free individual but also as an idea that must address social inequality. The idea of social equality is as universalizable as individual rights.

135 See https://eparlib.nic.in/bitstream/123456789/58338/1/ jcb_1951_constitution_1st_amendment_bill.pdf (accessed on 19 February 2022).

136 Ibid.

137 Burra, Arudra, 'Freedom of Speech in the Early Constitution: A Study of the Constitution (First Amendment) Bill', 2019, page 140, https:// www.researchgate.net/publication/331817430_Freedom_of_

speech_in_the_early_constitution_A_study_of_the_Constitution_First_Amendment_Bill (accessed on 19 February 2022).

138 Ibid., page 141.

139 Burra, Arudra, 'Civil Liberties in the Early Constitution: The *Cross Roads* and *Organiser* Cases', page 10, https://web.iitd.ac.in/~burra/research/burra19organiser-crossroads.pdf (accessed on 19 February 2022).

140 This was an exceptional episode of state violence. In February 1950, communist prisoners at the Salem Central Jail in Madras went on strike, demanding 'that they be treated as political detainees rather than as common criminals'. They 'refused to comply' with the protocols reserved for prisoners. When the policemen tried to make the communists 'revoke their strike and withdraw their demands', they resorted to violence which injured 'several policemen, including the deputy jailor'. In retaliation, the police trapped the '200-odd offenders in a hall with no means of escape' and opened fire. Twenty-two prisoners were killed and over a hundred injured. The episode reeks of the attitude of a colonial administration. Nehru was highly upset and spelt out in his correspondence with Sardar Patel that public opinion compared the police action with 'the British regime' [Singh, Tripurdaman, *Sixteen Stormy Days: The Story of the First Amendment of the Constitution of India*, Penguin India, New Delhi, 2020, pages 12–13].

141 Burra, 'Civil Liberties in the Early Constitution, page 10.

142 Ibid., page 14.

143 Ibid.

144 Ibid., page 17.

145 Ibid.

146 Ibid., page 18.

147 Ibid., page 19.

148 Chandrachud, Abhinav, *Republic of Rhetoric: Free Speech and the Constitution of India*, Penguin/Viking, 2017, New Delhi, page 75

149 Burra, 'Civil Liberties in the Early Constitution'.

150 Menon, Nivedita, 'Citizenship and the Passive Revolution', *Economic and Political Weekly*, Vol. 39, Issue No. 18, 1 May 2004, https://www.epw.in/journal/2004/18/special-articles/citizenship-and-passiverevolution.html (accessed on 19 February 2022).

151 Ibid.

152 Burra, 'Civil Liberties in the Early Constitution'.

153 Chandrachud, *Republic of Rhetoric*, page 79.

154 Ibid., page 81.

155 Ibid.

156 Burra, 'Freedom of Speech in the Early Constitution', pages 144–145.

157 Ibid., page 145. (My emphasis.)

158 Nehru *Letters for a Nation*, page 47.

159 Burra, Arudra, 'Arguments from Colonial Continuity: The Constitution (First Amendment) Act, 1951', Princeton University, 2008, page 32, https://deliverypdf.ssrn.com/delivery.php?ID= 29208409212107508707000006407712411903508802501602700909600312507509503007500807001006203206103400800902311202509810012308007804709101105205110212012111310011809603100106205502411410309309808702300209612100206502511802506900000902601307307500403107808083&EXT= pdf&INDEX=TRUE (accessed on 19 February 2022).

160 Singh, *Sixteen Stormy Days*, page 176.

161 Chandrachud, *Republic of Rhetoric*, page 80.

162 Crocker, Walter, *Nehru: A Contemporary's Estimate*, Vintage, Delhi, 2008, page 131.

163 Rushdie, Salman, *Imaginary Homelands: Essays and Criticism 1981–1991*, Penguin Books, New York, 1992, page 396.

164 Ibid.

165 See Guterres, António (foreword), 'United Nations Strategy and Plan of Action on Hate Speech', May 2019, https://www.un.org/en/genocideprevention/documents/UN%20Strategy%20and%20Plan%20of%20Action%20on%20Hate%20Speech%2018%20June%20SYNOPSIS.pdf (accessed on 19 February 2022).

166 Ibid.

Chapter 3: Culture, and the 'Urge towards Synthesis'

1   Nehru, Jawaharlal, *The Discovery of India*, Oxford University Press, New Delhi, 1964, p. 61 [friend and historian Sharmadip Basu made me pay attention to this example].

2   Ibid.

3   Ibid.
4   'Watch: TM Krishna Sings "Hum Dekhenge" in Four Languages at Shaheen Bagh in Delhi', *Scroll*, 8 February 2020, https://scroll.in/video/952525/watch-tm-krishna-sings-hum-dekhenge-in-four-languages-at-shaheen-bagh-in-delhi (accessed on 19 February 2022).
5   Nehru, *The Discovery of India*, , page 62.
6   Ibid.
7   Jäger, Friedrich, and Wiskind, Ora, 'Culture or Society? The Significance of Max Weber's Thought for Modern Cultural History', *History and Memory*, Vol. 3, No. 2 (Fall–Winter, 1991), pages 118–120.
8   Ibid., page 121.
9   Ibid.
10   Nobre, Renarde Freire, 'Culture and Perspectivism in Nietzsche's and Weber's View', translated by Bruno M.N. Reinhardt, *SciELO Social Sciences* English Edition, Teor. soc. Vol. 2. No. se Belo Horizonte 2006, http://socialsciences.scielo.org/scielo.php?script=sci_arttext&pid=S1518-44712006000200006&lng=en&nrm=iso (accessed on 19 February 2022).
11   Weber, Max, *The Protestant Ethic and the Spirit of Capitalism*, translated by Talcott Parsons, Routledge Classics, New York, 2001, page xxxv.
12   Weber's theory for India is that the caste system gives 'no indication that by themselves they could have created the rational enterprise of modern capitalism' [Weber, Max, *The Religion of India: The Sociology of Hinduism and Buddhism*, translated and edited by Hans H. Gerth and Don Martindale, The Free Press, Illinois, 1958, page 113]. Romila Thapar finds this thesis unhistorical and Orientalist. She interestingly mentions 'the Islamic ethic' exemplified in the Bohras and Khojas of Gujarat as responsible for introducing what is called 'incipient capitalism' in the seventeenth and eighteenth centuries [Thapar, Romila, *Cultural Pasts: Essays in Early Indian History*, Oxford University Press, New Delhi, 2000, page 46]. Despite Thapar's critique, Weber's thesis that cultural influences facilitate historical change, is vindicated.
13   Ibid.
14   Nehru, *The Discovery of India*, page 50.

15 Ibid.

16 Ibid., page 59.

17 Bhabha, Homi K., ed. *Nation and Narration*,, Routledge, New York, 1990, page 1.

18 Anderson, Benedict, *Imagined Communities*, Verso, London, 1983.

19 Nehru, *The Discovery of India*, page 518. (My emphasis.)

20 Ibid., page 59.

21 Speaking of China in the modern context, Nehru was naive in his time about communist China's ambitions, as his correspondence with Sardar Patel shows. Patel, in his letter to Nehru on 7 November 1950, draws from what he calls '[recent] and bitter history' to conclude that 'communism is no shield against imperialism and that the communists are as good or as bad imperialists as any other' [Hussain, Adeel, and Singh, Tripurdaman, *Nehru: The Debates That Defined India*, Fourth Estate, New Delhi, 2021, Kindle edition]. Making a distinction between Western imperialism and 'Chinese irredentism and Communist imperialism', Patel held that the latter 'has a cloak of ideology that makes it ten times more dangerous' [Hussain, and Singh, *Nehru: The Debates That Defined India*]. The recent and bitter history Patel mentions is perhaps China's occupation of Tibet in 1949. The communist states of China and the Soviet Union displayed expansionist tendencies. The erstwhile USSR invaded Czechoslovakia in 1968 and crushed what is called the 'Prague Spring'. In 1979, the Soviets invaded Afghanistan under the pretext of the new Soviet–Afghan Friendship Treaty. Nehru in a note of response on 18 November 1950, tried to allay Patel's fears. Nehru did not envisage a 'major attack on India by China', though he did consider 'gradual infiltration along our border . . . and taking possession of disputed territory' [Hussain, and Singh, *Nehru: The Debates That Defined India*]. In the end, a Himalayan border that was under dispute led China to attack India in 1962, thus blurring the line between infiltration and war. Nehru felt that Patel's suspicion that 'communism inevitably means expansion and war [and] that Chinese communism means inevitably an expansion towards India, is rather naïve' [Hussain, and Singh, *Nehru: The Debates That Defined India*]. Nehru's optimism regarding China turned out to be ironically naive. To Patel's fears about the access of literature and arms from China

and other communist nations, as a problem of 'internal security' [Hussain, and Singh, *Nehru: The Debates That Defined India*]. Nehru offers the democratic argument that the 'ideas are already there—and can only be countered by other ideas' [Hussain, and Singh, *Nehru: The Debates That Defined India*]. Citizens of a democracy reserve the right to have access to, and be influenced by, political ideas from across the world. The ethical (and political) limit to influence is the attempt to conspire against national sovereignty. To use the means of democracy to subvert it for undemocratic ends is not ethical.

22   Buber, Martin, *I and Thou*, translated by Walter Kaufman, Charles Scribner's Sons, New York, 1970, page 62.

23   Levinas, Emanuel, 'Martin Buber and the Theory of Knowledge', in *The Levinas Reader*, edited by Seán Hand, Basil Blackwell, U.K, 1989, page 66.

24   The point being made is that 'encounter is a better approximation of the meaning of *Begegnung*' (in the German original: Alles wirkliche Leben ist Begegnung), in *Encounters in Modern Jewish Thought: The Works of Eva Jospe*, Volume One: *Martin Buber*, edited by Raphael Jospe and Dov Schwartz, Academic Studies Press, Boston, 2013, page 13.

25   Levinas, 'Martin Buber and the Theory of Knowledge', page 66.

26   Hoskote, Ranjit, and Trojanow, Ilija, *Confluences: Forgotten Histories from East and West*, Yoda Press, New Delhi, 2012, Kindle edition.

27   Ibid.

28   Ibid.

29   Ibid

30   Kroeber, A.L., *An Anthropologist Looks at History*, edited by Theodora Koreber, University of California Press, 1963, Berkeley, Los Angeles, 1963, page 145.

31   Ibid., page 74.

32   Ibid., page 77.

33   Nehru, *The Discovery of India*, pages 518 (my emphasis) and 519.

34   Taylor, Charles, *The Sources of the Self: The Making of Modern Identity*, Cambridge University Press, Cambridge, Massachusetts, 1989, page 461.

35   Ibid., page 465.

36   Nehru, *The Discovery of India*, page 510. (My emphasis.)

37 Nehru, *The Discovery of India*, pages 518 (my emphasis) and 51.

38 Qurratulain Hyder's translation cited in Zakaria, Rafiq, *Indian Muslims: Where Have They Gone* Wrong?, Popular Prakashan, Mumbai, 2004, page 53.

39 Ibid., page 54.

40 Ibid.

41 Sen, Sudipta, *Ganga: The Many Pasts of a River*, Penguin/Viking Books, New Delhi, 2019, page 20.

42 Nehru, *The Discovery of India*, pages 518 (my emphasis) and page 115.

43 Ibid., page 122.

44 Ibid., page 155.

45 Ibid., page 156.

46 Biruni, Muḥammad ibn Aḥmad, *Alberuni's India* (v. 1), London: Kegan Paul, Trench, Trübner & Co., 1910, Columbia University Libraries Digital Collections, http://www.columbia.edu/cu/lweb/digital/collections/cul/texts/ldpd_5949073_001/pages/ldpd_5949073_001_00000089.html?toggle=image&menu=maximize&top=&left= (accessed on 19 February 2022).

47 http://www.columbia.edu/cu/lweb/digital/collections/cul/texts/ldpd_5949073_001/pages/ldpd_5949073_001_00000179.html?toggle=image&menu=maximize&top=&left=.

48 Nehru, *The Discovery of India*, page 136.

49 Kroeber, *An Anthropologist Looks at History*, page 62.

50 Nehru, *The Discovery of India*, pages 518 (my emphasis) and 136.

51 Ibid.

52 Ibid., page 155.

53 Ibid.

54 Ibid., page 216.

55 Ibid.

56 Ibid., page 520.

57 Ambedkar, Dr B.R., 'The Annihilation of Caste', in *Dr. Babasaheb Ambedkar Writings and Speeches*, Vol. 1, Education Department, Government of Maharashtra, Bombay, 1979, page 47.

58 Nehru, *The Discovery of India*, pages 518 (my emphasis) and 15.

59 Ibid. [Weber also notes in *The Religion of India*, that 'the typical Hindu deification process took its course first with regard to the

person of Buddha' (Weber, Max, *The Religion of India: The Sociology of Hinduism and Buddhism*, translated and edited by Hans H. Gerth and Don Martindale, The Free Press, U.S.A, Illinois, 1958, page 248).]

60   Ibid., page 77.

61   Ibid., page 146.

62   Ibid., pages 146–147.

63   Ibid., page 137.

64   Ibid., page 193.

65   Ibid., page 194.

66   Ibid., pages 195–196.

67   Ibid., page 196.

68   Ibid., page 198.

69   Ibid., page 259.

70   Ibid., page 269.

71   Ganeri, Jonardon, *The Lost Age of Reason: Philosophy in Early Modern India 1450–1700*, Oxford University Press, Oxford, 2011, page 25.

72   Ibid.

73   Ibid.

74   Ibid., page 268.

75   https://www.ramakrishnavivekananda.info/vivekananda/volume_6/epistles_second_series/142_friend.htm (accessed on 19 February 2022).

76   Nehru, *The Discovery of India*, pages 518 (my emphasis) and 161.

77   Ibid., page 245.

78   Ibid., page 73.

79   Weber, *The Religion of India*, page 20.

80   Ibid., page 117.

81   Nehru, *The Discovery of India*, page 74.

82   In his book, *In the Light of India*, Octavio Paz echoes Nehru's distinction between culture and religion: 'India, as a culture and as a history, is far greater than Hinduism, and thus Hindu nationalism lives in a permanent contradiction: its idea of Indian culture is religious; its vision of the Hindu religion entails its transformation into a political belief. The conversion of a culture into a religion ends with the conversion of a religion into politics' [Paz, Octavio, *In Light*

of India, translated by Eliot Weinberger, Harcourt, Inc., New York, 1995, page 116].

83   Ibid., page 59.
84   Paz, Octavio, 'Nehru: Man of Two Cultures and One World', in International Round Table on Jawaharlal Nehru, New Delhi, 1966, *Nehru and the Modern World*, Indian National Commission for Co-operation with UNESCO, New Delhi, 1967, page 13.
85   Ibid.
86   Ibid., page 14.
87   Nehru, *The Discovery of India*, page 564. (My emphasis.)
88   Ibid., pages 516–517.
89   Ibid., page 517.
90   Chatterjee, Partha, *Nationalist Thought and the Colonial World: A Derivative Discourse?* OUP, Delhi, 1986, page 133.
91   Ibid., page 134.
92   Ibid.
93   Ibid.
94   Ibid., page 138.
95   Ibid.
96   Ibid., page 139.
97   Ibid.
98   Nehru, *The Discovery of India*, page 519.
99   Ibid.
100 Ibid. ['There is something lacking in all this progress, which can neither produce harmony between nations nor within the spirit of man.']
101 Ibid., page 512.
102 Chatterjee, *Nationalist Thought and the Colonial World*, page 145.
103 Seth, Sanjay, 'Nehruvian Socialism—1927–37: Nationalism, Marxism, and the Pursuit of Modernity', *Alternatives: Global, Local, Political*, Vol. 18, No. 4, Fall, 1993, page 454.
104 Ibid., page 471.
105 Nehru, Jawaharlal, *India Today and Tomorrow*, Azad Memorial Lectures, 1959, Indian Council for Cultural Relations, 1960, page 13.
106 Kaviraj, Sudipta, *The Enchantment of Democracy and India: Politics and Ideas*, Permanent Black, New Delhi, 2018, Kindle edition.

[Kaviraj makes the important point that since Marxism finds democracy bourgeois and hence deceptive, while liberalism tends to treat democracy as 'ideologically uncriticizable as a political form . . . it is necessary to go beyond these two methods'.]

107 Nehru, *The Discovery of India*, pages 512–513. (My emphasis.)
108 Ibid., page 520.
109 Ibid., pages 519–520.
110 Ibid., page 512.
111 Ibid., page 35.
112 Ibid., page 324.
113 Ibid.
114 Ibid., pages 267–268.
115 Ibid., page 118.
116 Ibid.
117 See https://www.britannica.com/topic/purdah (accessed on 19 February 2022).
118 Nehru, *The Discovery of India*, page 41.
119 Ibid.
120 Thapar, Suruchi, 'Women as Activists; Women as Symbols: A Study of the Indian Nationalist Movement', *Feminist Review*, No. 44, Nationalisms and National Identities (Summer, 1993), page 81.
121 Ibid., page 89.
122 Ibid., page 83.
123 Ibid., page 86.

Chapter 4: History and the 'Roots of the Present'

1 Nehru, Jawaharlal, *India Today and Tomorrow, Azad Memorial Lectures*, 1959, Indian Council for Cultural Relations, 1960, page 7.
2 Nehru, Jawaharlal, *The Discovery of India*, Oxford University Press, New Delhi, 1964, page 23.
3 Baudelaire, Charles, *Selected Writings on Art and Literature*, translated by P.E. Charvet, Penguin Books, London, 1972, page 403.
4 Nehru, *The Discovery of India*, page 22.
5 Ibid., page 23.
6 Ibid., page 36.

7   Nietzsche, Fredrich, *The Use and Abuse of History*, translated by Adrian Collins, Bobbs-Merrill Company: Liberal Arts Press, New York, 1957 (second revised edition), page 51.

8   Ibid., page 52.

9   Nehru, *The Discovery of India*, page 21.

10 Ibid.

11 Hegel, Georg Wilhelm Friedrich, *Reason in History: A General Introduction to the Philosophy of History*, translated by Robert S. Hartman, The Bobbs-Merrill Company, New York, 1953, page 7.

12 Ibid., page 11.

13 The *Ramayana*, and the *Mahabharata*, Nehru wrote, gave the people 'a common background of heroic tradition and ethical living' [Nehru, *The Discovery of India*, page 100].

14 Hegel, Georg Wilhelm Friedrich, *Lectures on the Philosophy of World History*, Vol. 1, translated by Robert F. Brown and Peter C. Hodgson, Clarendon Press, Oxford, 2011, page 284.

15 Ibid., page 252.

16 Ibid., page 282.

17 Seth, Sanjay, 'Reason or Reasoning? Clio or Siva?', *Social Text*, 78, Vol. 22, No. 1 (Spring 2004), Duke University Press, page 90.

18 Chatterjee, Partha, *Nationalist Thought and the Colonial World: A Derivative Discourse?* Oxford University Press, Delhi, 1986, page 150.

19 Ibid., page 151.

20 Nehru, *The Discovery of India*, page 509.

21 Ibid., page 506.

22 Ibid.

23 Paz, Octavio, *Conjunctions and Disjunctions*, Arcade Publishing, New York, 1990, page 50.

24 Nehru, *The Discovery of India*, page 52.

25 Ibid., page 517. (My emphasis.)

26 Ibid., page 44.

27 Ibid., page 554.

28 Weber, Max, *From Max Weber: Essays in Sociology*, edited by H.H. Girth, C. Wright Mills, Routledge, New York, 2009, pages 356–357.

29 Nehru, *The Discovery of India* , pages 554–555.

30 Nehru, Jawaharlal, *Glimpses of World History*, Asia Publishing House, Bombay, 1962, page 6.

31   Ibid.
32   Ibid.
33   Ibid.
34   Ibid.
35   Ibid., page 13.
36   Ibid., page 22.
37   Ibid.
38   'BJP Makes a Delayed U-Turn, Modi Says Kumbh Attendance Should Now Be "Symbolic"', 17 April 2021, https://thewire.in/politics/covid-19-kumbh-mela-narendra-modi-symbolic (accessed on 19 February 2022).
39   Márquez, Gabriel García, Mendoza, Plinio Apuleyo, translated by Ann Wright, *The Fragrance of Guava*, Verso, London, 1982, page 111.
40   Ibid.
41   Nehru, *The Discovery of India*, page 33.
42   In the last section of *Chernobyl Prayer*, Svetlana Alexievich traces the traumatic experiences of the hazardous radiation from the explosion of the nuclear reactor at Chernobyl on 25–26 April 1986 by letting children speak: 'I had a friend, Andrei. They did two operations on him and then sent him home. Six months later he was supposed to get a third operation. He hanged himself from his belt, in an empty classroom . . . "We'll die, and then we'll become science," Andrei used to say. "We'll die and everyone will forget us," Katya said.' The fear of turning into a scientific object of enquiry, cast out of the world's memory, is a process of dehumanization [Alexievich, Svetlana, *Voices from Chernobyl: The Oral History of a Nuclear Disaster*, translated by Keith Gessen, Picador, New York, 2006, page 220].
43   Nehru, *The Discovery of India*, page 289. (My emphasis.)
44   Ibid., page 104.
45   Ibid., pages 102–103.
46   Ibid., page 103. (My emphasis.)
47   Ibid., pages 237–238.
48   Chattopadhyay, Brajadulal, *Representing the Other?: Sanskrit Sources and the Muslims (Eighth to Fourteenth Century)*, Manohar Publishers and Distributors, New Delhi, 1998, page 16.

49   Tagore, Rabindranath, 'Nationalism in the West', *Nationalism*, with
     an introduction by Ramachandra Guha, Penguin Books, New Delhi,
     2009, page 37.

50   Anderson, Benedict, *Imagined Communities*, Verso, London, 1983,
     page 5.

51   Nehru, *The Discovery of India*, pages 562–563.

52   Paz, Octavio, 'Nehru: Man of Two Cultures and One World',
     in International Round Table on Jawaharlal Nehru, New Delhi,
     1966, *Nehru and the Modern World* (New Delhi: Indian National
     Commission for Co-operation with UNESCO, 1967, page 16.

53   Chatterjee, Partha, *Nationalist Thought and the Colonial World: A
     Derivative Discourse?* OUP, Delhi. 1986, page 132.

54   Nehru, *The Discovery of India,* page 104

55   M.S. Golwalkar wrote: 'The Race Spirit has been awakening. The
     lion was not dead, only sleeping. He is rousing himself up again and
     the world has to see the might of the regenerated Hindu Nation strike
     down the enemy's hosts with its mighty arm' [Golwalkar, M.S, *We or
     Our Nationhood Defined*, Bharat Publications, Nagpur, 1939, page
     52]. This zoological imagination of race is reminiscent of W.B. Yeats'
     metaphor in the poem 'The Second Coming', of the lion with a man's
     head (which again strikingly resembles the image of the man-lion, or
     'Narsimha', found in Hindu mythology). The lion symbolizes the race-
     spirit out to destroy the race-enemy. Acknowledging the territorial
     zeal of the Nazis, Golwalkar observed that 'for a people to be and to
     live as a Nation, a hereditary territory . . . is essential' [Ibid., page 64].
     Race and territory, then, are the two complimentary, and overlapping,
     circles that define the right-wing idea of a nation. Carl Schmitt makes
     the argument in *The Concept of the Political* (1932) that constitutional
     democracy evades—does not have the guts—to name the enemy and
     understand politics for what it is: a friend–enemy binary, an idea
     retained in the modern era by fascism and communism. No wonder
     Golwalkar blamed the Indian National Congress, for 'letting our race
     spirit to fall asleep' and that it 'has been the root cause of our present
     unhappy condition . . . of hugging to our bosom our most inveterate
     enemies and thus endangering our very existence [Ibid., page 129].
     The political logic seems to be: democracy must be abandoned in
     order to drive out the nation's enemies. According to Foucault, the

history of the modern revolutionary project as well as its counter-history are implicated in devising a concept of war against the 'unity of the sovereign law that imposes obligations' [Michel Foucault, *Society Must Be Defended: Lectures at the College De France, 1975–76*, edited by Mauro Bertani and Alessandro Fontana, translated by David Macey, Picador, New York, 1997, page 70], or any state of law, or law of the state. The concept of war, like the concept of race and enemy, has no obligation to democracy. The picture is complete with Foucault's mention of Marx's letter to Engels in 1882, where Marx confesses that 'we found our idea of class struggle . . . in the work of the French historians who talked about the race struggle' [Ibid., page 79]. The idea of society comes into danger at this point. If society's prime historical motive is to wage war within, the idea of society is destroyed.

56   Yeats, W.B., *The Collected Poems of W.B. Yeats*, Wordsworth Poetry Library, London, 2000, page 159.

Select Bibliography

Alexievich, Svetlana. *Voices from Chernobyl: The Oral History of a Nuclear Disaster*. Translated by Keith Gessen. Picador. New York, 2006.

Ambedkar, Dr B.R. *Dr. Babasaheb Ambedkar: Writings and Speeches*, Vol. 1. Education Department, Government of Maharashtra. Bombay, 1979.

Ambedkar, Dr. B.R. *Dr. Babasaheb Ambedkar Writings and Speeches*, Vol. 2. Education Department, Government of Maharashtra. Bombay, 1982.

———. *Pakistan or the Partition of India*. In *Dr. Babasaheb Ambedkar: Writings and Speeches*, Vol. 8. Government of Maharashtra. Bombay: 1990.

Anderson, Benedict. *Imagined Communities*. Verso. London, 1983.

Anderson, Perry. *Indian Ideology*. Verso. New York. Kindle edition, 2021.

Appadurai, Arjun. *Fear of Small Numbers: An Essay on the Geography of Anger*. Duke University Press. Durham and London, 2006.

Asad, Talal. 'Modern Power and the Reconfiguration of Religious Traditions'. Interview with Saba Mahmood. *SEHR*, Vol. 5, Issue 1: Contested Polities, 27 February 1996.

Asif, Manan Ahmed. *The Loss of Hindustan. The Invention of India*. Harvard University Press. London, 2020.

Basu, Upmanyu. 'The Forgotten Exodus—Conflict of Kashmir Valley and Kashmiri Pandits'. *The Geopolitics*, 11 October 2020. https://

thegeopolitics.com/the-forgotten-exodus-conflict-of-kashmir-valley-and-kashmiri-pandits/.

Baudelaire, Charles. *Selected Writings on Art and Literature*, translated by P.E. Charvet. Penguin Books. London, 1972.

Benjamin, Walter. *Illuminations: Essays and Reflections*, translated by Harry Zohn and edited by Hannah Arendt. Schocken Books (Random House Inc.). New York, 1969.

Bhabha, Homi K. *The Location of Culture*. Routledge Classics. New York, 1994.

———. ed. *Nation and Narration*. Routledge. New York, 1990.

Bhargava, Rajeev. 'Should Europe Learn from Indian Secularism?' *Seminar*, 2011.   https://www.india-seminar.com/2011/621/621_rajeev_bhargava.htm.

Bhattacharjee, Manash Firaq. 'We Foreigners: What It Means to Be Bengali in India's Assam'. *Aljazeera*, 26 February 2020. https://www.aljazeera.com/features/2020/2/26/we-foreigners-what-it-means-to-be-bengali-in-indias-assam.

Bilgrami, Akeel. 'Two Concepts of Secularism'. *Economic and Political Weekly*, Vol. 29, No. 28, 9 July 1994.

Bocock, Robert. 'The Cultural Formations of Modern Society'. In *Modernity: An Introduction to Modern Societies*, edited by Stuart Hall, David Held, Don Hubert and Kenneth Thompson. Wiley-Blackwell. Oxford, 1996.

Breton, André. *First Manifesto of Surrealism in Art in Theory 1900–1990: An Anthology of Changing Ideas*, edited by Charles Harrison and Paul Wood. Oxford: Blackwell Publishers, 1992.

Buber, Martin. *I and Thou*, translated by Walter Kaufman. Charles Scribner's Sons. New York, 1970.

Burra, Arudra, 'Arguments from Colonial Continuity: The Constitution (First Amendment) Act, 1951'. Princeton University, 2008. https://deliverypdf.ssrn.com/delivery.php?ID=29208409212
10750870700000640771241190350880250160270090960
03125075095030075008070010062032061034008009023112025098100123080078047091011052051102120121113100118096031001062055024114103093098087023002096121002065025118025069000009026013073075004031078083&EXT=pdf&INDEX=TRUE.

———. 'Civil Liberties in the Early Constitution: The *CrossRoads* and *Organiser* cases'. https://web.iitd.ac.in/~burra/research/burra19organiser-crossroads.pdf.

———. 'Freedom of Speech in the Early Constitution: A Study of the Constitution (First Amendment) Bill'. 2019. https://www.researchgate.net/publication/331817430_Freedom_of_speech_in_the_early_constitution_A_study_of_the_Constitution_First_Amendment_Bill.

Carpentier, Alejo. 'On the Marvelous Real in America'. *Magical Realism: Theory History. Community*, edited by Lois Parkinson Zamora and Wendy B. Faris. Duke University Press. Durham & London, 1995.

Chakraborty, Dipesh. *Habitations of Modernity*. The University of Chicago Press. Chicago, 2002.

———. 'Postcoloniality and the Artifice of History: Who Speaks for "Indian" Pasts?' *Representations*, No. 37, Special Issue: Imperial Fantasies and Postcolonial Histories, Winter, 1992. Published by University of California Press.

Chandrachud, Abhinav. *Republic of Rhetoric: Free Speech and the Constitution of India*. Penguin/Viking. New Delhi, 2017.

Chatterjee, Partha. 'Ambedkar's Theory of Minority Rights'. In *The Radical in Ambedkar: Critical Reflections*, edited by Suraj Yengde and Anand Teltumbde. Gurgaon: Penguin India/Allen Lane. New Delhi, 2018.

Chatterjee, Partha. *The Nation and Its Fragments: Colonial and Postcolonial Histories*. Princeton University Press. Princeton, New Jersey, 1993.

———. *Nationalist Thought and the Colonial World: A Derivative Discourse?* Oxford University Press. Delhi, 1986.

Chattopadhyay, Brajadulal. *Representing the Other? Sanskrit Sources and the Muslims (Eighth to Fourteenth Century)*. Manohar Publishers and Distributors. New Delhi, 1998.

Chisick, Harvey. 'Ethics and History in Voltaire's Attitudes toward the Jews'. *Eighteenth-Century Studies*, Vol. 35, No. 4, Summer, 2002. The Johns Hopkins University Press.

Crocker, Walter. *Nehru: A Contemporary Estimate*. Vintage. Penguin-Random House. New Delhi, 2008.

Defoe, Daniel. *A Journal of the Plague Year*, with an introduction by Jason Goodwin. Modern Library. New York, 2001.

Derrida, Jacques. *The Politics of Friendship*, translated by George Collins. Verso. London, 1997.

Fareed, Rifat. 'The Forgotten Massacre That Ignited the Kashmir Dispute'. *Aljazeera*, 6 November 2017. https://www.aljazeera.com/news/2017/11/6/the-forgotten-massacre-that-ignited-the-kashmir-dispute.

Foucault, Michel. *Society Must Be Defended: Lectures at the College De France. 1975–76*, edited by Mauro Bertani and Alessandro Fontana, and translated by David Macey. Picador. New York, 1997.

Freud, Sigmund. *The Uncanny*, edited by David Mclintock. Penguin Books. London, 2003.

Ganeri. Jonardon. *The Lost Age of Reason: Philosophy in Early Modern India 1450–1700*. Oxford University Press. Oxford, 2011.

Gilmour, David. *The British in India: A Social History of the Raj*. Picador. New York, 2019.

Godse, Nathuram. *Why I Killed Gandhi*. Srishti Publishers & Distributors. New Delhi, 2020.

Golwalkar, M.S. *We or Our Nationhood Defined*. Bharat Publications. Nagpur, 1939.

Gunn, T. Jeremy. 'Do Human Rights Have a Secular, Individualistic and Anti-Islamic Bias?' Daedalus, Vol. 149, No. 3, 2020.

Hall, Stuart. 'The West and the Rest'. *Modernity: An Introduction to Modern Societies*, edited by Stuart Hall, David Held, Don Huburt and Kenneth Thompson. Blackwell. Oxford, 1996.

Hegel, Georg Wilhelm Friedrich. *Lectures on the Philosophy of World History*, Vol. 1, translated by Robert F. Brown and Peter C. Hodgson. Clarendon Press. Oxford, 2011.

————. *Reason in History: A General Introduction to the Philosophy of History*, translated by Robert S. Hartman. The Bobbs-Merrill Company. New York, 1953.

————. *Philosophy of Right*, translated by S.W. Dyde, Cosmo Classics. New York, 2008.

Heidegger, Martin. *Identity and Difference*, translated by Joan Stambaugh. Harper & Row. New York, 1969.

Hoskote, Ranjit, and Ilija Trojanow. *Confluences: Forgotten Histories from East and West*. Yoda Press. New Delhi. Kindle edition, 2012.

Jafferlot, Christopher. *The Hindu Nationalist Movement and Indian Politics: 1925 to the 1990s*. Hurst & Company. London, 1996.

Jäger, Friedrich, and Ora Wiskind. 'Culture or Society? The Significance of Max Weber's Thought for Modern Cultural History'. *History and Memory*, Vol. 3, No. 2, Fall–Winter, 1991.

Jayal, Niraja Gopal. 'Faith-Based Citizenship: The Dangerous Path India Is Choosing'. *The India Forum*. Issue: 1 November 2019. https://www.theindiaforum.in/article/faith-criterion-citizenship.

Kaviraj, Sudipta. *The Enchantment of Democracy and India Politics and Ideas*. Permanent Black. New Delhi. Kindle edition, 2018.

———. 'Modernity and Politics in India'. *Daedalus*, Vol. 129, No. 1. Multiple Modernities, Winter, 2000.

Khilnani, Sunil. *The Idea of India*. Penguin India. New Delhi, 2004.

———. 'Nehru's Faith'. *Economic and Political Weekly*, Vol. 37, No. 48, 30 November–6 December 2002.

Kimura, Makiko. *The Nellie Massacre of 1983: Agency of Rioters*. Sage Publications. New Delhi, 2013.

Kolsky, Elizabeth. 'The Colonial Rule of Law and the Legal Regime of Exception: Frontier "Fanaticism" and State Violence in British India'. *The American Historical Review*, October 2015.

Kosambi, D.D. *Combined Methods in Indology and Other Writings*. Oxford University Press. New Delhi, 2002.

Kroeber, A.L. *An Anthropologist Looks at History*, edited by Theodora Koreber. University of California Press. Berkeley and Los Angeles, 1963.

Kundera, Milan. *Immortality*, translated by Peter Kussi. Harper Perennial Classics. New York, 1999.

Levinas, Emanuel. 'Martin Buber and the Theory of Knowledge'. In *The Levinas Reader*, edited by Seán Hand. Basil Blackwell. Oxford, 1989.

Levinas, Emanuel. *Otherwise Than Being: Or Beyond Essence*, translated by Alphonso Lingis. Duquesne University Press. Pittsburg, Pennsylvania, 1981.

———. *Totality and Infinity: An Essay on Exteriority*. Martinus Nijhoff Publishers. The Hague, 1979.

Malraux, André. *Anti-Memoirs*, translated by Terance Kilmartin. Holt, Rinehart and Winston. New York, 1968.

Márquez, Gabriel García and Plinio Apuleyo Mendoza. *The Fragrance of Guava*, translated by Ann Wright. Verso. London, 1982.

Menon, Nivedita. 'Citizenship and the Passive Revolution'. *Economic and Political Weekly*, Vol. 39, Issue No. 18, 1 May 2004. https://www.epw.in/journal/2004/18/special-articles/citizenship-and-passiverevolution.html.

Nag, Sajal. 'Nehru and the Nagas: Minority Nationalism and the Post-Colonial State'. *Economic and Political Weekly*, Vol. 44., No. 49, 5–11 December 2009.

Nandy, Ashis. 'Cultural Frames for Social Intervention: A Personal Credo'. *Indian Philosophical Quarterly*, Vol. 11, No. 4., October 1984.

Nehru, Jawaharlal. *An Autobiography*. Oxford University Press. New Delhi, 1980.

———. *The Discovery of India*. Oxford University Press. New Delhi, 1964.

———. *Glimpses of World History*. Asia Publishing House. Bombay, 1962.

———. *Letters for a Nation: From Jawaharlal Nehru to His Chief Ministers 1947–1963*, edited by Madhav Khosla. Penguin India. New Delhi, 2014.

———. 'The Panorama of India's Past'. *Seminar*, 2018. https://www.india-seminar.com/2018/704/704_from_nehru's_writings.htm.

Nietzsche, Fredrich. *The Use and Abuse of History*, translated by Adrian Collins. Bobbs-Merrill Company: Liberal Arts Press. New York, 1957 (second revised edition).

Nobre, Renarde Freire. 'Culture and Perspectivism in Nietzsche's and Weber's View', translated by Bruno M.N. Reinhardt. *SciELO Social Sciences English Edition*. Teor. soc. vol.2 no.se Belo Horizonte, 2006. http://socialsciences.scielo.org/scielo.php?script=sci_arttext&pid=S1518-44712006000200006&lng=en&nrm=iso.

Noorani, A.G. *The Destruction of Hyderabad*. Tulika Books. New Delhi, 2013.

Paz, Octavio. *The Labyrinth of Solitude*, translated by Lysander Kemp, Yara Milos and Rachel Phillips Belash. London, 1985.

———. *In Light of India*, translated by Eliot Weinberger. Harcourt. Inc. New York, 1995.

———. 'Nehru: Man of Two Cultures and One World'. In International Round Table on Jawaharlal Nehru. New Delhi, 1966. *Nehru and the Modern World*. New Delhi: Indian National Commission for Co-operation with UNESCO, 1967. https://archive.org/details/in.ernet.dli.2015.159218/page/n15/mode/2up?q=octavio+paz+nehru&view=theater.

Rimbaud, Arthur. *Collected Poems*, translated by Martin Sorell. Oxford University Press. New York, 2001.

Roy, Anupama. *Mapping Citizenship in India*. Oxford University Press. New Delhi. Kindle edition, 2010.

Rushdie, Salman. *Imaginary Homelands: Essays and Criticism 1981–1991*. Penguin Books. New York, 1992.

Rushdie, Salman. *Shame*. Vintage. London, 1995.

Sandel, Michael. 'The Procedural Republic and the Unencumbered Self'. *Political Theory*, Vol. 12. No. 1, February 1984.

Savarkar, Vinayak Damodar. *Hindutva: Who Is a Hindu?*. Veer Savarkar Prakashan. Savarkar Sadan. Bombay, 1969.

Schmitt, Carl. *Political Theology: Four Chapters on the Concept of Sovereignty*, translated by George Schwab. MIT Press. Cambridge, Massachusetts, 1985.

Sen, Sudipta. *Ganga: The Many Pasts of a River*. Penguin/Viking Books. New Delhi, 2019.

Seth, Sanjay. 'Nehruvian Socialism—1927–37: Nationalism, Marxism, and the Pursuit of Modernity'. *Alternatives: Global, Local, Political*, Vol. 18, No. 4, Fall, 1993, pages 453–473.

———. 'Reason or Reasoning? Clio or Siva?'. *Social Text* 78, Vol. 22, No. 1, Spring, 2004. Published by Duke University Press.

Siddique, Nazimuddin. 'A Response to Hiren Gohain: The NRC Is a Product of Xenophobia in Assam'. *Economic and Political Weekly*, Vol. 55, Issue No. 14, 4 April 2020. https://www.epw.in/engage/article/response-hiren-gohain-nrc-product-xenophobia-assam.

Singh, Tripurdaman. *Sixteen Stormy Days: The Story of the First Amendment of the Constitution of India*. Penguin. New Delhi, 2020.

Singh, Tripurdaman, and Adeel Hussain. *Nehru: The Debates that Defined India*. Fourth Estate. New Delhi. Kindle edition, 2021.

Tagore, Rabindranath. *Nationalism*, with an introduction by Ramachandra Guha. Penguin Random House. New Delhi, 2009.

Taylor, Charles. *The Sources of the Self: The Making of Modern Identity*. Cambridge University Press. Cambridge, Massachusetts, 1989.

Tejani, Shabnum. 'The Necessary Conditions for Democracy: B.R. Ambedkar on Nationalism. Minorities and Pakistan'. *Economic and Political Weekly*, Vol. 48. No. 50, 14 December 2013.

Tejani, Shabnum. *Indian Secularism: A Social and Intellectual History. 1890–1950*. Permanent Black. Delhi, 2007.

Thapar, Romila. *Cultural Pasts: Essays in Early Indian History*. Oxford University Press. New Delhi, 2000.

———. *The Penguin History of Early India: From he Origins to AD 1300*. Penguin Books. New Delhi, 2002.

Thapar, Suruchi. 'Women as Activists; Women as Symbols: A Study of the Indian Nationalist Movement'. *Feminist Review*, No. 44. Nationalisms and National Identities, Summer, 1993.

Weber, Max. *From Max Weber: Essays in Sociology*, edited by H.H. Girth and C. Wright Mills. Routledge. New York, 2009.

Weber, Max. *The Protestant Ethic and the Spirit of Capitalism*, translated by Talcott Parsons. Routledge Classics. New York, 2001.

Weber, Max. *The Religion of India: The Sociology of Hinduism and Buddhism*, translated and edited by Hans H. Gerth and Don Martindale. The Free Press. Illinois, 1958.

Yeats, W.B. *The Collected Poems of W.B. Yeats*. Wordsworth Poetry Library. London, 2000.

Zakaria, Rafiq. *Indian Muslims: Where Have They Gone Wrong?* Popular Prakashan. Mumbai, 2004.

Index